Poems

Angelo Lumelli

Poems

Edited by Eugenio Gazzola
Translated by Gianpiero W. Doebler

Agincourt Press
New York, 2024

Opuntia is an imprint of Agincourt Press
Luigi Ballerini and Gianluca Rizzo, Editors
Agincourt Press is a non-profit organization chaired by Berardo Paradiso

© 2024 by Agincourt Press
First published in Italian as *Le poesie*
© 2020, Edizioni del Verri, Milan

All manuscripts are subject to peer review.

All rights reserved.

ISBN: 978-1-946328-40-3

AGINCOURT PRESS
P.O. Box 1039
Cooper Station
New York, NY 10003
www.agincourtbooks.com

Table of Contents

7 *Destination and Origin: An Introduction to Angelo Lumelli's Work*
by Eugenio Gazzola

oblivion / oblivion (2020)
  26 senti l'antifona / get the hint
  30 motivetto / catchy tune
  38 refrain / refrain

vocalises / vocalises (2008)
  44 1. un'insistente variazione / 1. an insistent variation
  64 2. pause / 2. pauses
  72 3. sei facce di un cubo / 3. six faces of a cube
  76 4. vocalises / 4. vocalises

seelenboulevard / seelenboulevard (1999)
  86 1. come quando / 1. like when
  90 2. barbara celarent / 2. barbara celarent
  94 3. sasso piatto / 3. flat stone
  98 4. silent / 4. silent

bambina teoria / child theory (1990)
  104 1. un moccioso chiede di te / 1. a brat asks for you
  110 2. duo soledad / 2. duo soledad
  118 3. il trapezista che volò / 3. the trapeze artist who flew
  126 4. decennio / 4. decade
  130 5. oh voi dormienti angeli / 5. oh you sleeping angels

trattatello incostante / variable treatise (1980)
138 1. raccontino da fermo / 1. little story standing still
150 2. imitazioni e preghiere / 2. imitations and prayers
170 3. trattatello incostante / 3. variable treatise
178 4. candid camera / 4. candid camera

cosa bella cosa / thing beautiful thing (1977)
184 1. a un millimetro dal corpo (chi ti trova?) / at a millimeter from the body
186 2. all'uscita del cinema / 2. upon leaving the movies
188 3. passerotto mio caro piumoso / 3. my dear feathery little sparrow
190 4. apri l'uscio apri l'uscio / 4. open the door open the door
192 5. potrebbe essere quella la scena / 5. that could be the scene
194 6. c'era da aspettarselo / 6. it was to be expected
196 7. incomprensibile borotalco fine fine / 7. incomprehensible very fine talcum powder
198 8. siliqua sistro sonaglio / 8. sistrum rattle silicles
200 9. si sente il colpo del tram / 9. if you hear the bump of the tram
202 10. in assenza del fatto / 10. in the absence of the deed
204 11. chioschetti delle angurie / 11. little watermelon stands
206 12. il lavandino al piano di sopra / 12. the washbasin on the next floor up
208 13. chi teneva così lucide / 13. those who kept the handles
210 14. vedi quel fatto laggiù? / 14. see that thing down there?
212 15. corpi dove vanno così belli / 15. bodies where do they go so beautiful
214 16. alcune cose alle spalle / 16. a few things behind you
216 17. erano risposte premature / 17. they were premature responses
218 18. ci sono altre descrizioni possibili / 18. there are other possible descriptions
220 19. sequestrato in altre storie in famiglie / 19. sequestered within other stories
222 20. illimitati esterni / 20. unlimited exteriors
224 21. eppure - sono sicuro / 21. and yet – I am sure
226 22. non posso competere / 22. I can't compete
228 23. non sono fatti / 23. they are not done
230 24. l'universale non verrà / 24. the universal will not come

233 *The revolving door of the Hotel Excelsior*

Destination and Origin: An Introduction to Angelo Lumelli's Work

by Eugenio Gazzola

Angelo Lumelli's new book is the result of the rewriting of his poetic work. The author has defined the operation as a "re-statement," which amounts to a new saying, an ever-losing struggle against the irrecoverable, the return to uncertainty, to its enormous and unsatisfied faith, to the nascent word, child of the voice. With that, it's a blowing up of one the few sure things in literature, the fateful "text," which is all the more sacred and untouchable when, having become a "figure," it requires not being disfigured. Instead, a careful work of excavation, removal, and substitution has collided with the pages of the past—even the recent past—leaving them new. He saved only the titles: *thing beautiful thing, variable treatise, child theory*, and *seelenboulevard*.[1] Thus, it is an unpublished book, and it is a book of life.

1. The Re-Statement of the Text

Let's take two poems and compare their openings in the two versions: the first publication and the current one. We begin with "decade," a poem included in 1990's *child theory*:

```
[1990 version]
finally
nothing will be      different enough
therefore neither I  nor scattered objects
the old cupboard will have to
neither wait         nor call
```

---

[1] With the single exception of *for not being the water that I love* [*per non essere l'acqua che amo*] (La Vita Felice), which has become *vocalises*.

> in the ecstasy of shadow and dust
> instead it will call
> in the bags of chickpeas   rattles quiver
> […]
>
> [2020 version]
> in the end
> there will be nothing   different enough
> storehouse of lights and powders
> there's the pump for the sulfur
> a bag of copper sulphate
> in the universe of eyelids in motion
> everything is in a safe place
> everything is immortal
> there's the bread   in its bag on the table
> the flour   with two eggs beside it
> […]

Here, the key to everything seems to reside in the verse: "nothing will be different enough" that in the two versions is stated with different intentions. In the text from 1990, the "different enough" seems to also include the subject, disoriented among the remains of an event and their reawakening. In the text from 2020, on the other hand, an everlastingness of the event is verified, attested to by the beating of the eyelids, which in their partial closure remain witnesses and believers: "everything is in a safe place / everything is immortal."

The second opening is taken from "little story standing still" which opens *variable treatise* [*trattatello incostante*]:

> [1980 version]
> I lack the heart
> (I am letting you know)
> I am here to appear
> I must manage myself
>
> (therefore, it isn't amicable or only
> from now on that which I say
> exclusive is my not touching
> here pretended divisible
> but you can't count on it)

[2020 version]
at least let it seem to me, city
like your empty Sunday streets
the pathways of the sky that repeat: everything that exists
is fuel on the flames!
let me participate, I ask,
with all my parentheses closed
(hey it's me – I'll finally tell you)
(I am the air under your skirt)
words with which
I've beaten myself for so long
like the window that slams
while not even a wisp of air blows.

In this case, we have before us two completely different poems, of which the first (1980) poses a political and rhetorical question—one of religious ethics, really—regarding poetry's aspiration to be dialogue—almost as if dialogue were the sole justification of poetry. In the text from 2020, however, we follow the process that Lumelli himself defines elsewhere as "the upended knitting":[2] from the inside of the knitting comes all the desire for the real, without obstacles, as if the determination in invoking it constituted the basis of the dialogue, and so poetry enters into itself in the same moment it exits toward things, toward the beautiful Sunday events, the wide roads, the startling of a window slamming without a breath of air blowing—or rather, everything that was hidden in the poem from 1980, precisely in its opposite.

More generally, at the time of *variable treatise*, the poet prepares a certain position toward "things in themselves," an old and undying demon of poetry. The desire for dialogue and exclamation is strengthened; inwardness is always searching for the "open." It's between the naturalistic Lombard line and that of

---

[2] This image of upended knitting is one we find often in Lumelli's work, up to the most recent, "The revolving door of the Hotel Excelsior" ["La porta girevole dell'Hotel Excelsior"], from 2020: "My task is to provide the error, subjected to justification, bringing forth wreckage. // This is why, every time, I have upended the text's knitting through childlike curiosity, through incredulity, through penitence—thwarting the hard face of the expression to find the mysterious appeal, without the protection of outside facts, without exclusive and ruinous histories confronting the cry of the mind. // The upended knitting has allowed me to imagine a world that does not deny what it hides, that preserves its incredible reserve of figures, that loves its accomplices, the knots and threads that dangle, the nape of the neck—I would dare say, my maternity." (243).

Savoyard crepuscularism that there finally comes forth a beginning in the dazzling American light of *Early Sunday Morning* by Edward Hopper. A framing halfway between family intimacy and the city that moves forward. Figures that know each other so well that they avoid each other. They are found on "Sunday morning," and what makes their common life real is concentrated there in that waiting for clarity, which is left hanging.

Now, if there is one stable element—just one in the mechanism of poetry—it is precisely the *given*, the writing through which the reader comprehends. But when Lumelli *re-states* and rewrites his work, it is certain that he gets rid of it. In some ways, he takes it away and moves it to a subsequent time: from the past he jumps to the present, so that the *re-statement* leads to overturning the "natural" order of reading of all the work stretched out fully, which at this point loses its chronological extension and ends up being combined with the present. It becomes a single work that continually revives itself from a certain point onward, while the word *that is working* takes the place of the word *given* once and for all. The statement, with its semblance of being up to date, the dawn of language, becomes a highly symbolic gesture that recognizes a living function in language itself, continued from and alerted to all of the poet's experience as it gradually re-emerges, starting from childhood.

Lumelli, then, can consider today's text final not because it is finished, but because the time is finished. If he were to allow himself once again to open the closed door of the event, new words would be added to the old.

This is the reason why, above, we defined this as a book of life.

With the twentieth century, it became clear to everyone that poetry is work about poetry. It's that way in its essence, not through goodwill. In 1970, Adriano Spatola wrote in *Tam Tam* that, "poetry is the problem of poetry." And among the first, Paul Valery, at the beginning of that century and in the wake of the beloved Mallarmé, expressed an idea of poetry already fully understood in the work of germination and formulation of the text, instead of in the result—that is, poetry in its mental beginning and its never-finished process.[3]

In particular, the idea of process has distinguished Lumelli's work for almost fifty years, a work that has ripened along the crest between two centuries,

---

[3] In Valery, there is one of the principles that guides both the psychological and literary analysis of the text, starting, I believe, from the first of the *Cahiers* (1925), see *Quaderni I*, Adelphi, 1985.

holding together gains and losses like a *scar*—that is, back and forth with the measured and repeated gesture of the needle and thread, until the split is closed. There is a ritual undercurrent in this always-equal moment that, over the course of time, holds together and keeps tied.

The question of time—early, late—is a crucial theme in Lumelli's writing.

> time calls me at the end of the hall – I didn't understand anything
> it tells me: you must move forward without jumping
> I tell him that he's telling lies – that he wants to make me arrive late
> shall we make a bet? he tells me
> you'll see that I'll beat you – I tell him: we'll see
> when I get there it's no longer me.
> [From "pause," in *vocalises*, 65]

The verses refer to the suspended time of childhood and elementary school, when a child's courage is also measured in the mythical struggle between language and its priests—for example, the teacher who, as we read in the closing, "this is why truth follows him – it walks quickly / with the skirt with the slit / it runs after them tottering on glass heels." But the decisive time of being seems to be an empty time or a time of waiting that presents itself through riddles (*that he wants to make me arrive late*) instead of offering itself as time carried out—and time that will require being "skipped" in order to get somewhere.

Lumelli lets a long coexistence with the masters of the German language show through, particularly with Friedrich Hölderlin and Georg Trakl.[4] This reveals, paradoxically, a deeply Italian poet—most of all, in a certain obsessive sensibility with respect to ruins, to the remains of the landscape, of impressions and fragments of a whole that has been lost.

And Italian, I believe, is his frequent practice of *visitation*—in reality, an act of appropriation during which he tries to put those ruins and fragments back together according to another plan and with cinematographic imagination, cutting and reassembling successive frames. His poetry is largely composed of places—for the most part, places of invocation that request a frequent mental return, perhaps a revision of fact as happens in pilgrimages by car on the mysterious streets of experience, from Valle Staffora to Val Tidone.

---

[4] An old interest dating from his university days to which a volume of several years ago attests: *Verso Höderlin e verso Trakl)*, (Coliseum series edited by Giorgio Albertazzi and Nani Cagnone, La Finestra Editrice, 2017).

Finally, there is the obsessive presence of an *addressee*, almost always invisible, to whom the poet speaks, preferably addressing and admonishing with *tu*, a sort of profile of guilt from which he solicits a response in vain.

2. The Course of Life[5]

Angelo Lumelli was born on 9 April 1943 in Ramata, a place with five or six houses in the Comune of Momperone in the Alexandrine Oltrepò, on the border between Piedmont and Lombardy.

But there is an episode regarding the border of which it is nearly obligatory to make use. In 1943, Momperone had been annexed as a *frazione* to the Comune of Bragnano Frascata, following incorporations that had occurred during the fascist era. It turns out, then, that Lumelli—whose house he never moved away from—was born in the Comune of Brignano Frascata, but only until 1946, or until Momperone regained its autonomy as a *commune*. We are thus authorized to hold his birth registration as the first case of *rewriting* that he encountered. Further, in the spare biographical jacket flaps of his book, Lumelli himself never cites Momperone, but rather La Ramata, where really lives, at the top of the hill.[6]

Lumelli is a fantastic narrator. In conversation with him, one gets countless details: atmospheres, hours of the day, or the passage of a bird that becomes essential to his story, precisely because it is extraneous. But the facts are the threshold of the words, and so much precision, so much abundance of details, makes one lose sight of the context. The detail is magnified, and the story withdraws.

For example, in order to understand that, as a boy, he spent his high school ears in a seminary—an interval the biographer would judge relevant—he preferred to look out the window of a tall and austere building into the valley below, where dozens of bulldozers, excavators, and trucks were working on construction of the Genova-to-Milan highway, the future A7. This is what he saw

---

[5] I relate here some information that Lumelli himself supplied me with on the occasion of an interview with the author released in January 2020.

[6] "The place from which one looks cannot, never ever, claim to be in view. Why can't you stand it? I asked him once. I had no response, but I felt that he was about to cry" [*bianco è l'istante*, Milano: edizioni del verri, 2005: 21].

from the Seminary of Stazzano, on the eve of an escape without regrets. Lumelli summarizes the long seasons at the school in a final way, but on the other hand, he expands episodes within an hour, making them cover decades. Several years later, we find him in Germany studying the language of the philosophers, acting really like a migrant on the trains from Southern Italy, arriving in Munich at six in the morning. Returning to Italy to become a middle school teacher, starting in Confienza, amid the rice fields of Vercelli which he still loves from having heard them talked about by his mother and father, who worked in the rice-producing countryside.

From 1970 to 1980, he lived in Milan in a two-room apartment at Via Col di Lana 6. In 1980, he finally returned to Ramata where, at the persuasion of several friends, he also served as mayor. He founded and managed, for twenty years, an agricultural cooperative that he no longer wants to talk about but whose "things" he describes, as if in a screenplay: the big Piedmontese cattle, the cultivation of 100,000 strawberry plants, the aging of the salami with religious care for their white and gray mold. The reason Lumelli speaks of things in this case, and never of people, could be revenge (or sadness) for the end of a utopia that lasted twenty years. And he tells of how, in the mid-1980s, he began collaboration with an engineering society that specialized in EU planning and scheduling in the agricultural field, writing thousands of pages of plans, many more than the pages of his novels, which ended up remaining poor. He tells of his travels to Brussels in a car with Emilio Rapetti, a great expert in agriculture, passing one-by-one, along secondary roads, the old apple trees of Europe—the only distraction and an unforgettable generosity for his eyes.

And against this backdrop, we understand how writing has never been an easy house for him to inhabit, one from which he has continued to enter and exit every day of his whole life, as if to demonstrate that language is not a place, but an aspiration. Now that he dedicates himself to it entirely (but he says it with dismay), it's as if he had met a girl for the first time.

This is where the uneasiness that never leaves his writing originates. And it becomes visible only from time to time, as happens in "motivetto," the second part of the unpublished *oblivion* (2020). There's a point of fracture in the word there, and it is the point of absolute correctness, when the word does something; it is embodied in the subject we are discussing:

> like a hero I saw you amid language in ruins while it fell to pieces here and there with a cry and dark gurgling phonemes in the tracheas mend-

> ed as well as possible I saw you with your arms raised as in a mortified embrace – imploring given up, I in this fake storm – amid a swarm of questions you gnats of syllables! waiting for the great phrase to utter as if it were discovering America!
> [from "motivetto," in *oblivion*, 33]

If we question Lumelli about the identity of this dramatic character, he will respond, but with difficulty, that it is about his brother: "All bodies collapse in the midst of language. Their end, while language continues to speak, also marks the destiny of every word: harmless, limited, burdened with that about which it remains silent. The figure that, ahead of all others, represents the individual end is the figure of Giancarlo, my brother, who constantly accompanies me, taking me by the hand, toward justice. Since we were children, in my sleep, I played the concave part, which he embraced; that gesture of bliss became a painful hollow. He died in 1979, at the age of 33, on the dark night of 3 November, the eve of his birthday. Facing a dead body, poetry can only bounce off. In the form of a rebound, the tightrope-walking appearance of the fall, it can rise in its own circus and, on the trapeze, try the number that can make it live. I've written somewhere that my poor family is my etymology, like Sanskrit."

3. Milan, Via Col di Lana 6

In the 70s, Milan was a beloved place for Lumelli, the reservoir of life and its charms.

In "white is the moment" ["bianco è l'istante"] he describes it this way:

> In Milan there are streets directed toward the setting of the winter sun, something very refined and rare.
> This is the real magic: the city's space multiplies the south and north sides, it directs the winds, distributes the shadows.
> Thousands of people put their key in the lock and
> thousands of places exclude them, while the festival of
> solitudes begins.
> [...]
> In that moment, the gong is struck for a strange match: he who arrives in person first at the exchange.
> [*bianco è l'istante*, Italian edition, 12]

Milan is the connection. The city calls, and the poet becomes a part of it, an expanse of secrecy par excellence. Milan is a glimpsed skeleton, in the sense that at particular times, it lets its streets be seen extended along the road map and in the special light of its neighborhoods, living paintings transformed into signs: "the feeling that it was following people / already passed Via Custodi // the bottom comes to the surface / in amusing little bubbles / aperitif / with so many canapés // [...]" from *thing beautiful thing* [*cosa bella cosa*].

In 1970, with the purpose of setting up a literary journal, a couple of friends displayed an announcement on a blackboard of the Università Statale. The response was overwhelming: they arrived by the dozens at Via Col di Lana 6. Among the many, a core group was created with Michelangelo Coviello and Milo De Angelis, while other friendships formed in those years: Silvio Giussani, Alberto Mari, Mario Mieli, the painter Giuseppe Lollo, and Piero Leddi, from Lumelli's province, whom he met in Milan.

The evenings in Via Col di Lana were dedicated to the reading of texts that each person wrote, readings that, it appears, were word-by-word, ruthless, and admirably destructive.

The group succeeded in also involving already established poets: Giancarlo Majorino, Antonio Porta, Giovanni Raboni, and even Franco Fortini offered to listen, taking them seriously. Trips were undertaken to Bologna, where more avant-garde criticism was concentrated (Renato Barilli, Fausto Curi, Guido Guglielmi, Giorgio Celli). Several years later, around the mid-1970s, a fortunate meeting for Lumelli occurred with Nanni Cagnone and Luigi Ballerini.

His debut was in 1977 with a collection entitled *thing beautiful thing* [*cosa bella cosa*], issued by the publisher Guanda. The book already contained, condensed into a crystal through slow release, all the themes that Lumelli's poetry had disclosed in other ways up to *oblivion*. The cover has a jacket flap written by Giancarlo Majorino with this opening: "Feet on the ground and head in flames, the beaten up and stubborn hero of these poems questions everything that is not *I*." The book won the Viareggio First Work prize, creating much embarrassment for Lumelli.

These were years in which Italian poetry was seeking a path to withdraw from a certain form of over-exposition of industrial society and from a political conflict that had become harsh. At the same time, on another front, an almost bizarre lyrical renaissance was developing—a last reaction to the avant-garde. But Lumelli did not participate in theoretical preambles. Challenges did not excite him, however much he was, in fact, jostled about between those who longed for a gradual rise toward a decisive word and those who aimed at a language in the midst of everything. Lumelli established himself at the crossing point, like a child exile or the young Jew of the verses of *oblivion*, as we shall see.

From the years of continuous reconsideration there comes to Lumelli the fragmentariness of his verse, the thin, quivering construction that recalls the architect Fausto Melotti, while everything passes by incessantly and occurs again. Just as happens today with his *rewriting*.

4. The Only Book of Poetry

We must consider the work we are presenting as his "only book of poetry," following Lumelli's own wishes. It is a book divided into six parts, written from about 1970 onward but offered in this volume in inverse chronological order, or starting from the last: *oblivion*, the most recent and never published in any format. It is difficult to say why a poem dedicated to memory, invoked as an only witness, carries this title. Memory carries with it images without protection, irrevocable, which result in a painful exaltation with the sort of hymn that characterizes the third and final composition in the collection, entitled *refrain* (39):

> [...]
>   if we were a herd
> with the wind on our skin   insatiable childhood
> that expects life   how many times
> faced with small things
> have we become immense   like those leaving
> a place   fanatics
> lost in an illegitimate sky
> does some garden with magnolias
> know something about us?
> [...]

Reading him, he seems to be traveling along the Highway of the Giovi[7] in the direction of someone who, coming from the passes of the Apennines, exits from

---

[7] Translator's Note: *Highway of the Giovi*: Autostrada A7, the main highway that runs between Milan to Genoa.

the curves to dash into wide roads, in the quiet landscapes that dominated the childhood Lumelli spent on those first hills between Piedmont and Lombardy.

What does it mean to go toward childhood? In an explicit way, the first two passages of "get the hint" ["senti l'antifona"] (27), set at the opening to *oblivion*, announce having undertaken the journey.

> phrase – our port on the high sea
> socks of rough wool
> scarves that prick the children's necks
> lists and broken windows on the west
> you – scrutinized detail
> and you – courageous schoolboys
> phrases – windows
> opening for pious men
> noses against the windows – little hands
> that wave bye-bye.
>
> here I am!
> like a frightened guy who's laughing
> supreme child
> the shot has no way back
> first syllable – that leaves you stunned?
> nativity – we might at least meet
> the eyes of a stranger –
> the passer-by who turns
> toward sons repeating a year.

If we finally try to follow it, this path toward childhood to which we are continually driven, page after page, we will come across a child who is following the path in the opposite direction, in the direction of the language that, like an explosive syllable, was lost at birth just when it became understood. That "supreme child" is captured in the moment of the explosion of the first syllable, that which launches the "dazed" journey of the return.

Is it toward that original explosion that every poet is bound?

Birth inaugurates the "short line," the existence that ends "against its wall," so the true investigation, the undertaking like Parsifal's, is *à rebours*, in the return to very small statement, to wailing and its insufficiency as an extreme point, but a *point sublime*.

Among the varied techniques of concealment and breaking free that Lumelli applies in a systematic way, there is the throwing out of a signal, a name, a cry that immediately dissolves. It's the technique of someone who hides in order to reveal, someone who covers up in order to signal, as the living do with the dead and as Christo did with veiled monuments.

Oblivion, for example, had another title. It was originally called *Papirosn*. It's useless to ask why the poet had chosen a *klezmer* tango of the 1920s, entitled *Papirosn*, inspired by a Jewish child who sells cigarettes on the street, to speak of loss and confusion. This note is useful only for recalling the phenomenon through which Lumelli always *rewrites* while he writes, as he grinds mythologies and old stories that no one remembers any longer. His is a compulsion to break loose, wanting to reveal a more ancient truth: age and days pass and carry us backwards, precisely as it seems that they push us forward.

Lumelli has written much about *making* poetry. But I think that someone seeking a reason or description of his work in prose would encounter difficulty—for example, the reliable topographical indication of a place evoked, a biographical fact, or a detail of concrete visualization, as common with Montale's riviera, Ungaretti's war, Balestrini's working masses, or even just with Adriano Spatola's il Mulino. It would a vain effort, because Lumelli makes any personal concrete fact that concerns him and his work seem trifling and irrelevant.

His copious prose writing is flowering with allegories and temporary extension of poetry. It is an uninterrupted verse that has changed pace, following the outline of a mountain, without intervals between the peaks' highs and the valleys' lows. In the same way, he follows an interior movement that is revealed on the threshold of visibility: in a flow of thoughts that experience stirs up, in which true things are given as a clue, a flake of snow that dissolves. The key that you expect, the story you see beginning, is immediately interrupted. The writing sinks and you lose sight of the story.

In 1980, in the self-introduction that opens *variable treatise*, Lumelli writes of himself: "I was born in southern Piedmont, among the secluded hills near the Apennines. Even today, the lands, if not the people, tend toward exclamation more than toward speech, and without the civic abstraction of the technique, oscillate between complete dedication and complete distance." And later (16): "Contemplating with timid firmness the very beautiful potatoes the generations that preceded me practiced their religion of effort while meaning flew off elsewhere, and the time of things began its cry, in secret."

As soon as he has had us capture the glint of real things—the hills and everything the landscape has nourished it with—as soon as we have glimpsed the biographical frame we were seeking, they are immediately and brusquely dissolved, pushing his own demons onto the scene. And so his lands, about which he would like to inform us, might become "exclaimed" speech, and they are transfigured on a plane of abstraction that he keeps at a distance. And the thought about the potatoes—which seems to me worthy of being recalled, in itself strong in evocation—evaporates in the secret cry of the things we will never hear. Again, unable to understand the whole, we are led to grasp only luminous fragments.

And yet there's a line, a phrase in that same *self-presentation*, that tells more about the earth and the poet's people than he wants us to know—because there is always something that eludes the watch of poets—when he says, "Sometimes I must have mistaken worry for thought," and here there leaps forth the fury of the language of experience. In fact, it is a popular declension that transforms worries into thoughts. "Having some thoughts [*avere dei pensieri*]" is said not of someone who creates horizons with thought, but of someone who is pursued, step by step, by a thought personified, by a shadow, one could say by a "sign"—that once again, in the dialectal vocabulary, signifies disgrace or destiny.

Observing the course of the poetry from *oblivion* (2020) to *cosa bella cosa* (1977), we note, finally, the movement we were speaking of a little earlier, that progress toward the end that, in reality, always leads to the beginning. This is how destination and origin coincide.

Writing becomes a race against time and against the final crumbling of its snapshots. Having perceived the risk that everything might again fall to pieces, precisely when it seemed to him he had found the thread of the story, the poet drops cadence and extends the writing into "continuous verse." We are speaking of *child theory* from 1990 and *seelenboulevard* from 1999:

> smallest childhood and strange beauty of the frost in the anesthesia of the mind a flight of leaves falls upon you the photos in black and white were left in a shoebox somewhere there's old plaster and verdigris shadows did someone plant the vines against the wall on a favorable day? like a cloud of gnats the minutes of the humble rise briefly and flop for the second time adieu! while in the sky an enormous dirigible passes like a fantastic

> added-value a flying idea about your hole of the beginning that starts to sing *we are the champions*?
> [from *like when* [*come quando*] in *seelenboulevard*, 87][8]

It seems that up to this moment, memory had been the agent of the present. Now it starts being the time to be re-encountered, the time that has taken the upper hand and must be re-felt, recalled, resaid. The exercise of memory is stated from the title of *barbara celarent* taken from the old syllogistic model from school:

> the whole chronological order must be completely redone even the birth that had premonitions of every sort it's enough to skip a transition and everything becomes impossible to find...
> [*barbara celarent*, in *seelenboulevard*, 91]

Having passed those years, after the underground and mineral texts, we could say, of *seelenboulevard*, conceptual brevity and traditional verse returns, even with rhymes.

These are poems numbered one by one that we find in "an insistent variation" ["una insistente variazione"], a chapter in *vocalises* (formerly *for not being the water that I love* [*per non essere l'acqua che amo*]), in which we see assembled, in succession, figures that are perhaps known (or believed to be), and a collection of moments that begins in a bocce ball field and ends in Piazza Cadorna. It is one of the days in which the poet asks for news and passes around the photographs kept in a shoebox.

But the game of finding is interrupted every time at the point of succeeding, because something ruins it.

> 1.8
> at the last minute the ultimate pearl
> slipped off without a follower
> the whole little necklace scattered away
> it seemed a thing that had been lost

---

[8] The shoebox is another recurring image in Lumelli's poetry. See, for example: "In the old photographs, the pose is stated in a candid way. You can see from the position of the bodies, facing the lens and the voice that must have said stop!, they reduce to immobility all the parts generally in motion, like their arms and legs, not to mention their eyes, which are always caught in flagrante" (*white is the moment* [*bianco è l'istante*], Italian edition, 65).

and yet it was the most daring move
a twisted thread
to be passed five times through your fingers.
[from "an insistent variation" ["un'insistente variazione"] in *vocalises*, 59]

Lumelli has defined this moment in his poetry—around 2008—as an homage to elementary school. There is certainly nostalgia for the kindness of the profession, for small handicrafts, the joy of rhyme like the joy of a return.[9]

And there reappears the great obstacle of the parenthesis, the saying carried by another saying, the saying that speaks by remaining quiet because of its position, because it is inscribed on a tablet. Parenthesis is the word spoken while one is walking:

4.1
[(for not being the water that I love
        will I then be its pebble?)   (gentle waves
                                                    ever farther away)]

[(the transparency may not win
  where neither you nor I
  will be able to see each other)]
[(pebbles
  may there not be hardness within you
  smoothed)
(you fruit of the method
  exile that marries us again)]
[from *vocalises*, 77]

---

[9] The figure of the teacher also appears many times in the poems, both as a weaning from the mother and as a mysterious advance on the woman. See, for example: "while they're drawing poppies – they wet the pencil with saliva / they spend the hours on their heads – never enough is the increasing red / the poppy is a party skirt. // looking back is forbidden – the teacher is standing behind you / tall thighs beneath her apron – with her thighs she prevents you from moving back" ("pause" 2.1, 65), or in "white is the instant": "It doesn't go well for the teacher when explaining in explicit terms that the verb to be, in logical analysis, is called copula."

5. The Destination of Origin

> Regarding me, places particularly come to mind. Perhaps because the true book was in the extension, in the catalogue, in the list.
> [from "Self-presentation," in *trattatello incostante*, 1980]

This passage works as a confession. Writing consists of the places that have formed the poet—the ones clear as the sun, stated with so much civic direction, and those written between the lines. The "true book" that Lumelli eyes in those few words, however enigmatic, is the effort of giving an origin and a destination to his own path, discovering in the end that the two addresses coincide with the journey's lands in which he lives and where four provinces, five dialects, and countless idioms intersect. In all his poetry, Lumelli has wanted to return there, precisely where to the place from which he started and into which he still sinks his personal "etymology." Language and writing modeled on the undulating but rugged line, hidden for long stretches, of the hills of Momperone, Ramata, Volpedo, and up to Varzi and then Val Trebbia—hills arranged with successive wings, as in the backdrop of a theatre. The poetry rewrites Ithaca continuously, incessantly.

The mythography of the everyday is the scale on which to measure, precisely, the *list* and the *extension* that he recalls in that passage from the *Self-presentation*—with the understanding that he is not speaking of geographical extension, but of space and of time at once—that is, the going and returning, each time with "increased" awareness. Turning the piazza of Momperone into a *peripato* and an osteria of the town into *Auerbach's tavern*.

Although he is a poet difficult to understand, Lumelli has not laid out a philosophical poetry during these forty-some years of writing. "There is a language that cannot speak; in fact, it wants only to happen" ("Self-presentation").

To those going through his pages for the first time, we would like to suggest as a guide, if they believe it, an instruction for reading: keep in mind that Lumelli is a *visiting* poet. That is to say, he is a poet who passes by and marks the roads. He tags *his* places like an angel might do with the doorjambs of the chosen. The very difficulty of some passages, the obscurity of some images that seem placed to guard the text, have their origin in a language that abandons itself to prophecy—perhaps the final result of the "clumsy prayer" that surfaces from his memories: "As a boy, they might have been a science or a song, but they stopped before that and became prayers. Then they became clumsy players" [ibid].

The poet has said that in the hiding places of his adolescent devotion, he undertook reading of *I nomi di Dio* [*The Divine Names*] by the Pseudo-Dionysius the Areopagite, the gnostic of the early Christian centuries, about which Hugo Ball says that "he intends without doubt to pass through the Areopagite converted by Paul of Athens."[10] The search for the names to attribute to God (since God has need of man to be said) is destined to develop in a circular way, repeatedly touching the same points and rising toward the most living, most certain word, but without ever succeeding in filling up the unsayable. The light remains empty. One hears there the hard and continuous work committed to a path that is impossible for it to complete and which, therefore, remains open: "how can the subject of the divine names be carried out, on our part, given that I am showing the transcendent Divinity, the being that, cannot be named and is superior to any name?"[11]

How can I find the absolute, pure name, if the absolute has no name, if it is lacking a name and at the same time supplied with every name? As the universal Cause, in fact, he is suited to "both the absence of every name and all the names of beings."

The origin of poetry is in the research that is always beginning again, with inexhaustible motion forward and only forward. I believe that the *saying* and the *resaying* (like the *writing* and *rewriting*) that have given structure to Lumelli's poetry come from that—that is, they are the intervals of one single, prolonged motion toward a naming that has always been unattainable.

Here, I believe, the circle of our experience within Angelo Lumelli's poetry can close. However, we will notice, in our hearts, that a certain game remains among the parts of the machinery.

e.g.
Piacenza
February 2020

---

[10] Hugo Ball, *Cristianesimo bizantino*, Adelphi, 2015.
[11] Dionigi Areopagita, *Circa i nomi divini*, in *Corpos Dyonisiacum*. [Italian translation edited by Enrico Turolla, La Vita Felice, 2014, 261 et seq.]

Note:

The work of rewriting and *re-statement*, to which Angelo Lumelli has exposed his work in verse, suggests adopting for this volume, which gathers in full all his poems for the first time, an arrangement that moves backwards in time. Therefore, we find at the beginning the unpublished and recent long poem, *oblivion* (2020), from which we will go back to the first published collection, *thing beautiful thing* [*cosa bella cosa*], from 1977. In this way, we are going along with a point of view that contemplates the confluence of the past in an *open time* that makes, of Lumelli's work, a continuum that is forever fresh.

oblivion / oblivion
(2020)

senti l'antifona

frase - nostro porto in alto mare
calze di lana grezza
sciarpe che pungono il collo dei bambini
elenchi e vetri rotti dell'ovest
tu - scrutato particolare
e voi - scolari coraggiosi
frasi - finestre
varco per uomini pietosi
nasi contro i vetri - manine
che fanno ciao ciao.

eccomi!
come uno spavento che ride
bambino supremo
non ha ritorno lo sparo
sillaba iniziale - che ti lascia stordito?
natività - almeno incontrassimo
gli occhi di un estraneo -
il passante che si volta
verso figli ripetenti.

get the hint

phrase – our port on the high sea
socks of rough wool
scarves that prick the children's necks
lists and broken windows on the west
you – scrutinized detail
and you – courageous schoolboys
phrases – windows
opening for pious men
noses against the windows – little hands
that wave bye-bye.

here I am!
like a frightened guy who's laughing
supreme child
the shot has no way back
first syllable – that leaves you stunned?
nativity – we might at least meet
the eyes of a stranger –
the passer-by who turns
toward sons repeating a year.

arrivati all'uscita
cristallo dell'inverno - si moltiplica
folla di luci - facce
di tante persone
ebreo per qualche motivo
bambino nell'angolo
topolino della fede
non tollera correzioni
la colpa d'espressione:
il tuo nudo corpo
ecco ciò che chiede!

dissidente frase - che si corica
come un pensiero alla pari
come una faccia nell'erba
a viva forza - primi piani
passione e pupille
palpebre chiuse
per non tentare
il fatto in purezza
che non ci vuole.

having reached the exit
crystal of winter – multiplying
the crowd of lights – faces
of so many people
a Jew for some reason
child in the corner
little mouse of the faith
cannot put up with corrections
the offense of expression:
your nude body
this is what he asks for!

dissident phrase – that lies down
like a thought
with its face in the grass
deep strength – first plans
passion and pupils
eyelids closed
in order not to attempt
the act in purity
that doesn't want us.

motivetto

commento che prolunga	andantino della festa
altre ragazze si ripetono	con i loro primi orecchini
dopo vent'anni	trovi chiuse le persiane
palline di canfora	nelle tasche dei cappotti

ci siamo resi vuoti per cavarcela ma è un vuoto non puro come un vuoto civetta - anche se togli tutti i soprammobili quando avremo un vero crepuscolo? - un altrove che non si mescola - netta linea della dogana celeste, riga dentata delle Alpi Cozie! - finisse il finto intero il tempo extra del nostro commento: noi che abbiamo in tasca il nostro portafortuna - da anni - il curioso labirinto di un nocciolo di pesca!

certo che avremmo voluto fare festa con tanti piccolissimi finali - mente che sobbalza allo schianto di un fiammifero! - rompe verdi squame il papavero - ehilà! che rossa sottanina - si sciolgono le cose belle come i nastrini dei regali - questa sciarpa di lana soffice è per te Anna Schiavi - da piegare come una palpebra cieca - mentre guardi dai vetri - per coprirti la nuca.

catchy tune

comment that prolongs	the *andantino* of the party
other girls are repeated	with their first earrings
after twenty years	you find the shutters closed
little balls of camphor	in the pockets of the overcoats

we were left empty from getting by but it's an impure nothingness like a decoy void – even if you take away all the knick-knacks will we have a real twilight? – an elsewhere that does not get jumbled – a clear line of the celestial customs, toothy row of the Cottian Alps! – may the fictitious whole the extra time of our comment come to an end: we who've had our good-luck charm in our pockets – for years – the curious labyrinth of a peach pit!

of course we would have wanted to celebrate with so many very small endings – mind that jumps at the crack of a match! – the poppy breaks green scales – hey! what a little red skirt – the beautiful things come undone like the ribbons of gifts – this soft scarf is for you Anna Schiavi – to fold like a blind eyelid – while you look from the windows – to cover the back of your neck.

se ti invito a convergere   verso di me
grande urto   almeno arrivassi!
quando il linguaggio fallì caddero molti birilli
arrivano nebbie di ottobre giorni per la farinata di ceci.

come un eroe ti ho visto in mezzo al linguaggio in rovina mentre cadeva a pezzi di qua e di là con grida e oscuri fonemi gorgoglianti nelle trachee ricucite alla meglio ti ho visto con le braccia alzate come un abbraccio mortificato - orante arreso, io in questa finta bufera - tra nugoli di domande voi mosche di sillabe! aspettando la grande frase da pronunciare come fosse scoprire l'America!

parabrezza di una piccola chiesa - andiamo in macchina nell'Alto Oltrepò - fosse femminile, sesso di tutte le cose - a metà dell'oblio abbracciate colline - non basta un paesaggio alla pari - nostro riassunto mai intero - ritentato abbraccio, corrotto - unilaterale è il nostro fuori - clamante dicente: succhiami tutti i colori.

if I invite you to converge	toward me
great bump	if you would only arrive!
when language failed	many pins fell
October's mists arrive	days for chick pea porridge

like a hero I saw you amid language in ruins while it fell to pieces here and there with a cry and dark gurgling phonemes in the tracheas mended as well as possible I saw you with your arms raised as in a mortified embrace – imploring given up - I in this fake storm amid a swarm of questions you gnats of syllables! waiting for the great phrase to utter as if it were discovering America!

windshield of a little church – we're driving by car in the high Oltrepò – as if it were feminine, sex of all things – surrounding hills halfway to oblivion – such a landscape is not enough – our summary never complete – an embrace tried again, corrupted – outside us everything is temptation – calling saying: absorb all my colors.

alberi e giardini	muro di cinta del vostro peccato
sotto alti simboli	noi piccoli indovini
brace che si agita	a un filo di fiato
ai piedi di qualcosa	naso per aria dei bambini.

da capo a piedi muro scritto e riscritto - e l'inconsapevole? - che si dimentica e lascia incisioni a casaccio? - e il nostro privato per passare la notte? - uomini e donne come tutto esaurito? - voi luci coltivate - inverno dei gioiellieri - sfaccettate in mille facce - noi rifratti di spigolo - ancora tiepidi torbidi a quest'ora - brancolanti sotto i muri delle scritte - ecco i nostri foglietti!

quando finisce il lontano è finito anche il viaggio - non è un buon segno questa mano che non si stacca - meglio se lanci un sasso poi corri - convalescente con brevi corsette - basta una prospettiva pro forma - come avessi le gambe buone - la tua ombra per terra, ai piedi della destinazione.

trees and gardens   boundary wall of your sin
beneath tall symbols   we little fortune-tellers
embers that stir   with a wisp of breath
at the feet of something   children's noses in the air.

wall written and rewritten from head to foot – and the ignorant one? – who forgets and leaves random cuts? – and our privacy for spending the night? – men and women as if everything were used up? – you, cultivated lights – winter of the jewelers – faceted with a thousand faces – we, refracted edgewise – still lukewarm murky at this hour – groping about under the walls of writings – here are our slips of paper!

when the distant ends the journey also ends – it's not a good sign this hand that does not break away – it's better if you toss a stone and then run – convalescent with brief jogs – a pro forma perspective is enough – as if you had good legs – your shadow on the ground, at the feet of the destination.

mi gò fai pasà le stelle   come granini di riso
t'ho cercata di notte e di giorno bela siura an t'ò mia truvà
mi g'avevi da dirti una cosa   una cosa che adess l'ò smentià
ti at g'avevi una treccina lunga longa   e con quella cordina mi tieni ligà.

ad alta voce vanno i vecchi dei ricoveri - con parole che hanno soltanto nomi e cognomi - dont ca t'è! dont ca t'è! - sulle dita ricordi a memoria - si scoraggia ciò che non passa di mano - trionfano piastrelle in questa piazza pulita - disinfettanti nel carrellino delle scope - mano posata sul tovagliolo - dialoghi soltanto in uscita - il dolorino dei sensi senza presa - artrite nelle nocche delle dita.

chiarezza troppo chiara - dita che si attaccano a un bottone - sole basso come i passettini di un infermo – oh il continuo, poi puntini puntini - al posto di detto e ridetto - l'odierno abitato, per tutto l'inverno!

I sifted through the stars   like grains of rice
I looked for you night and day   beautiful lady but I didn't find you
there was something I had to tell you something I have now forgotten
you had a very long pigtail   and with that rope you held me tied.

with raised voices the old people of the shelter come – with words that have only first and last names – where are you! where are you! – memories by heart on their fingers – disheartening that which falls from hands – tiles swept too cleanly – disinfectant in the broom cart – hand laid on the napkin – attempted dialogues by only one – small pain of the sense without a grip – arthritis in their knuckles.

clarity too clear – fingers fastening a button – low sun like the small steps of a sick man – oh the continuum, then dots, dots – in the place of said and resaid – inhabited every day, for the whole winter!

refrain

deficit di qualcosa
ruga di espressione
intorno agli occhi
ciò che sempre rammemora
(noi miseri del lontano
esplodono fiori gialli
invece che gonfi di pus
inaccessibili gioie
su potenti cardini
non per il loro aprirsi
ancora parliamo
fonte di calore incredibile
soltanto poiché vivi
quando con tenerezza
come una leggenda
autunno con alberi incendiati
di giallo e di rosso
con il vento nel pelo
che pretende la vita
davanti a cose piccole
siamo diventati immensi
di luogo
persi in un cielo illegittimo
quale giardino con magnolie
sa qualcosa di noi?
vuoti cortili con galline ovaiole
tovaglie bianche di domenica
torna liscia la superficie
ora che da sconvolto sapere
vorremmo stringerci le mani
una volta sola
zigomi riconosciuti nel buio
corpo con freddi genitali
con stuoli di zie
la scatola di latta dipinta a fiorami?
parte da zero
che cancella le date

antico appello
graziose zampe di gallina
midons
amor de lonh
macchie di un sogno)

crochi così puri
portate con onore
cielo di smalto
ma poiché respinti
di quei bisonti sotto la neve

ansimanti
raggiungiamo il comune sentire
brevi faville, veloci

fossimo mandria
incontentabile infanzia
quante volte

come usciti
fanatici

che abbiamo agitato

Ernesto
memorabile

fossimo tribù
dov'è finita

lo spirito infuriato
l'onomastico

refrain

deficiency of something
wrinkle of expression
around your eyes
that which always recalls
(we poor people from afar
yellow flowers explode
instead of swelling with pus
inaccessible joys
on strong hinges
not for their opening
we still speak
source of incredible warmth
only because living
when with tenderness
like a legend
autumn with trees aflame
with yellow and red
with the wind on our skin
that expects life
faced with small things
have we become immense
a place
lost in an illegitimate sky
does some garden with magnolias
know something about us?
empty courtyards with laying hens
Sunday's white tablecloths
it becomes smooth again the surface
now that from upset knowledge
we would like to shake hands
just once
cheekbones recognizable in the dark
body with cold genitalia
with a host of aunts
the tin box painted with a flowered pattern?
starting from zero
that erases the dates

age-old plea
pretty crow's feet
midons
amor de lonh
sketches of a dream)

saffron so pure
carried with honor
glazed sky
but since they are pushed back
of those bison in the snow

panting
we attain common feeling
brief sparks, rapid

if we were a herd
insatiable childhood
how many times

like those leaving
fanatics

that we disturbed

Ernesto
memorable

if we were a tribe
where did it end up

the enraged spirit
the name day

nel secolo banale   mancata vestizione
dei morti   con i vestiti della festa
corpi che furono monumenti
arrivati in miseria   davanti a figli confusi
cosa fa il presente da solo?
si sente un tic tic di cesoie
chi pota le viti a quest'ora?
se tu comparissi come un forestiero
come un ospite verso sera
non ancora interrogato   bello
come un'impresa
una pura lingua straniera   tu vedresti
come sono stato fermo sul posto
ho aspettato la stellina di ogni sera
come all'antica   all'era dei buoi
con il novecento che c'insegue
perfino nelle vigne   lavorate all'uncinetto
sulla neve   il presente fa la voce grossa
ma uno per uno   erano i minuti
nostre pupille in moto   misteriosa bambina
scacciata in una donna
mia etimologia   vocali resi lucide dall'uso
sassolini sonanti   in noi
lingua ostinata
senza conciliazione   sia invece
grido della nascita - che   una volta almeno
ci riconosca.

in the unimportant century
of the dead
bodies that were monuments
that became destitute
what will the present do by itself?
the *snip snip* of shears can be heard
who is trimming the vines at this hour?
if you appeared as a stranger
like a guest near nightfall
not yet questioned
like an undertaking
a pure foreign language
how I have remained in place
I waited for every night's little star
like they used to do
with the twentieth century pursuing us
even into the vineyards
in the snow
but one by one
our pupils in motion
driven away into a woman
my etymology
resonant pebbles
stubborn language
without reconciliation
a birth cry – that
recognizes us.

lacking dressing
with their best clothes

faced with confused children

beautiful

you would see

in the time of the oxen

crocheted
the present speaks loudly
were the minutes
mysterious girl

vowels rendered shiny through use
within us

may it instead be
at least once

vocalises / vocalises
(2008)

1. un'insistente variazione

1.1
il pergolato sopra il gioco delle bocce
m'interroga e io gli rispondo
siamo tu ed io gli dico
c'è un muro color verderame
c'è una sedia di ferro arrugginito
ci fu il colpo secco sul pallino
un altro bersaglio fu colpito
passarono scarpette di vernice
due gambe fino all'orlo della gonna
il mondo restò a terra
sotto il cielo dell'assunta
sulla cima dei suoi seni
tutto fu rapito
uomini con il cappello
accompagnano le bocce
con la testa coperta sotto l'infinito.

1. an insistent variation

1.1
the pergola over the bocce ball game
asks me and I respond
it's you and me I tell him
there is a verdigris-colored wall
there is a chair of rusty iron
with one clean stroke the *pallino* was hit
once again a target was struck
little patent leather shoes passed by
two legs up to the hem of her skirt
the world remained on the ground
under the Madonna's heaven
up to the peak of her breasts
everything was raised
men with their hats
accompany the bocce balls
covered heads beneath the infinite.

1.2
non uno degli innumerevoli
nemmeno uno per fare una partita
alla fine ho visto un incompiuto
che ogni tanto mi guardava
carta di un gioco sconosciuto
qua la mano ho detto
e ho visto la mia che mancava.

1.2
not one of the innumerable
not even one to have a match with
finally I saw an incomplete one
who now and then was looking at me
card of an unknown game
let's shake hands I said
and I saw mine which was missing.

1.3
a volte basta mettersi in coppia
uno a destra uno a sinistra
spingere avanti le cose
come mandare a letto i pulcini
non c'era nessuno soltanto noi due
chi ha detto che è davvero accaduto?
ogni piccola cosa la fa grande il suo vuoto
talvolta nel cuore si accende una spia
come l'assenza che non va via.

1.3
sometimes it's enough to pair them up
one on the right one on the left
push things forward
like sending the chicks to bed
there wasn't anyone just us two
who said that it really happened?
its void makes every little thing become big
sometimes in my heart a warning light goes on
like the absence that doesn't go away.

1.4
ci pensò un arcangelo alla fine
a sottrarlo dal linciaggio della folla
lo liberò come un palloncino
come la bambina
che balla sulle punte
trasfigurato in un lampo
sfigurato sul ring
a braccia aperte
come una conquista
ruppe il filo di lana
fuori dalla pista.

1.4
an archangel finally thought about it
rescuing him from the lynching of the mob
he freed him like a balloon
like a little girl
who dances on her toes
transfigured in a flash
disfigured in the ring
with arms open
like a conquest
he broke the woolen thread
off the track.

1.5
gli rimase il salto con l'asta
un istinto animale
come la volpe che non si fida
il passero che non osa dormire
saltava con gli occhi senza palpebre
ostacoli visti nell'aria
ombre del cuore
il buio che brilla
un balzo invisibile
un lampo nella pupilla
un baleno che salta un dolore
un salto di niente
diventato un mestiere
come un punto d'onore.

1.5
the pole jump remained for him
an animal instinct
like the fox that doesn't trust
the sparrow that dares not sleep
he leapt with his eyes without eyelids
obstacles seen in the air
shadows of the heart
the darkness that shines
an invisible jump
a spark in his eye
a flash that leaps over a pain
a nothing leap
having become a craft
like a point of honor.

1.6
non so chi interrogò per primo
se io o loro
eccomi! risposi in anticipo
alla domanda di nessuno
crollato io per primo
nel gioco da bambino
mentre giravano
domanda e risposta
come a nascondino.

1.6
I don't know who asked first
if it was me or them
here I am! I answered early
to no one's question
I collapsed first
in the game as a child
while there spun around
question and answer
like in hide-and-seek.

1.7
passano al volo soluzioni
come palloncini nelle fiere
non sempre scoppiano
qualcuno vola via
sembrava tutto tranquillo
tra i passanti in piazza Cadorna
ma tutti interrogavano
nella folla senza sosta
anch'io chiedo in giro
se sono io la risposta.

1.7
solutions go by right away
like balloons at the fair
they don't always burst
a few fly away
everything seemed quiet
among the passers-by in Piazza Cadorna
but everyone was asking
in the crowd without stopping
I also ask around
whether I am the answer.

1.8
all'ultimo minuto l'ultima perlina
senza la seguente si sfilò
si disperse l'intera collanina
sembrava una cosa perduta
ma fu la mossa più ardita
un filo di refe
da passare cinque volte nelle dita.

1.8
at the last minute the ultimate pearl
slipped off without a follower
the whole little necklace scattered away
it seemed a thing that had been lost
and yet it was the most daring move
a twisted thread
to be passed five times through your fingers.

1.9
forse un arcangelo potrà
accendere quell'attimo
senza ricompense
noi soltanto con dolore
nell'impurità dei motivi
torbido istante
che cade a fagiolo
ma soltanto una volta
sia concesso esclamare
teoria che non sa competere
con la nostra compassione
prestigiatore mille dita
coniglietto della ragione.

1.9
perhaps an archangel would be able
to kindle that moment
without recompense
we only with pain
in the impurity of motives
cloudy moment
that falls at just the right time
only once
may it be allowed to exclaim
theory that cannot compete
with our compassion
a thousand-fingered magician
bunny rabbit of reason.

1.10
da mirabili spaventi
un piccolo buongiorno
anima che porta gonne a fiori
compagne di scuola
vanno sui tacchi
lontane dall'infanzia
ginocchia nascoste
muovono il vestito
c'è il non fatto
per non farlo sparire
secchi cardi
nella fiamma dei venti
splende il nulla
che fa bene alle cose
ponticelli di minuti
come parole sospese
oh righe degli indovini
cadono lacrime oscure
sui quaderni bagnati dei bambini.

1.10
from wonderful frights
a little *buongiorno*
soul that wears flowered skirts
girls at school
going about on heels
far from childhood
knees hidden
they move the clothing
there's what isn't done
so as not to make it disappear
dry thistles
in the flame of the winds
the nothing shines
that does good for things
little bridges of minutes
like suspended words
oh lines of the fortune-tellers
while dark tears fall
on the children's wet notebooks.

2. pause

2.1
mentre disegnano papaveri - bagnano la matita con la saliva
passano le ore sulla testa - aumenta il rosso che non basta
il papavero è una gonna della festa.

indietro è vietato guardare - la maestra sta in piedi alle spalle
alte cosce sotto il grembiule - con le cosce impedisce di arretrare.

luogo preferito - detriti dove crescono sambuchi
soffio di scuri scantinati - bambine e giubbini sbottonati
guardaroba con lo specchio - anta girata e rigirata
stanza capogiro - mente di continuo rovesciata.

oh madri delle nascite incomplete - del buco dietro la nuca
io della grammatica che aiuta - io da dire io che risbuca
nello specchio si specchia la luna - meno male che cambia la scena
lucente padella luna piena.

il tempo stava in fondo al corridoio - ti aspetto
mi dice da lontano - ho preso la rincorsa
per saltare dieci anni – la Gilera ha vinto il campionato
io sono un duro e non mi giro – ho detto tre volte lo giuro.

mentre piangevo scendeva il moccio dal naso
il tempo contava i millenni - mescolava le carte nel mazzo
la maestra passa tra i banchi - forse mi sfiora i capelli
appoggio il viso alla sua gonna - lei dice che la colpa è mia
che l'ho fatta grossa – e mi sono voltato.

il tempo mi chiama in fondo al corridoio - non hai capito niente
mi dice: tu devi avanzare ma senza saltare
io gli dico che dice bugie - che vuole farmi arrivare in ritardo
facciamo una scommessa? mi dice
vedrai che ti metto nel sacco – io gli dico: staremo a vedere
quando arrivo non arrivo più io.

2. pauses

2.1
while they're drawing poppies – they wet the pencil with saliva
they spend the hours on their heads – never enough is the increasing red
the poppy is a party skirt.

looking back is forbidden – the teacher is standing behind you
tall thighs beneath her apron – with her thighs she prevents you from moving back

favorite place – detritus where elder trees grow
a whiff of cellar shadows – girls and little unbuttoned coats
wardrobe with the mirror – door turned and turned again
room dizziness – continually overturned mind

oh mothers of incomplete births – from the hole behind the nape
I of the grammar that helps – I from saying I who re-emerges
in the mirror is reflected the moon – thank heavens it changes scene
shining skillet full moon.

time stood at the end of the hall – I'm waiting for you
it tells me from afar – I do a run-up
to leap ten years – Gilera won the championship
I'm a tough guy and don't turn back – I swear I said three times.

while I was crying some snot fell from my nose
time counted the millennia – shuffled the cards in the deck
the teacher passes between the benches – perhaps she brushes against my hair
I rest my face on her skirt – she says it's my fault
that I made a big mistake – and I turned away.

time calls me at the end of the hall – I didn't understand anything
it tells me: you must move forward without jumping
I tell him that he's telling lies – that he wants to make me arrive late
shall we make a bet? he tells me
you'll see that I'll beat you – I tell him: we'll see
when I get there it's no longer me.

il tempo si è arrabbiato davvero – lascia ore senza le ore
forse non viene più sera
il cielo non vuole cambiare - allora mi cambio da solo
parole con altre parole.

nobili pirati conoscono il mestiere - hanno in testa fazzoletti a quadretti
sul tempo ci vanno a cavallo - gli passano sopra con grandi velieri
non vengono presi sul fatto - raccontano che dappertutto è lontano
che qui è più lontano di tutto.

per questo la verità gli va dietro - cammina svelta
con la gonna con lo spacco
li rincorre traballando sui tacchi di vetro.

time really got mad – he left hours without the hours
maybe evening won't come any more
the sky doesn't want to change – then I changed on my own
words with other words.

noble pirates know their trade – they have checkered kerchiefs on their heads
using the time they go by horse – they cross over with great sailing ships
they aren't caught by surprise – they tell how everywhere is far
but here is farthest of all.

this is why truth follows him – it walks quickly
with the skirt with the slit
it runs after them tottering on glass heels.

2.2

a botta calda uno dice complimenti a malerbe e macerie che sballano il sistema gerarchico ma chi si lamenta dell'innumerevole? polverosi cespugli di more mettono la pulce nell'orecchio c'è un'osteria a Lacchiarella dove fanno ceci con le cotiche dove si può trovare una piccola rima con qualcosa con lima con stima con prima e tanti saluti.

è la fine che scatena la retorica e il bell'epilogo delle periferie lo stile patetico oh urbs pulcherrima che innalza (pardon!) quella peroratio di facciate come in fondo a Lorenteggio balconi che guardano marcite per fortuna voi centri mai trovati! dalla verità mancati! qui vagano bellezze furiose con jeans a vita bassa escono ragazze e motorini arriva un'ora dolce e malvagia nel marasma dell'io pomeriggi al cinema e seni bambini annaspano stivaletti con le stringhe nelle utilitarie si appannano i vetri oh tabernacolo segreto scala verso dio! mentre l'essere mostra la sua fodera di seta.

vanno fatti a concludere affari meno male che i secoli hanno lasciato labirinti in faccia al mare meno male che c'è Genova in extremis con le madonne nelle nicchie dei muri le cupole che si gonfiano quando il sole comincia a tramontare nel caos del vello d'oro pesanti farfalle alzano e abbassano ali di muco se calcoli ore e minuti il 98% è fatto di attese oh il semplice mare! che è complesso senza darlo a vedere! mente che spegne le sue gemme per togliere le offese!

vertigine che aleggia sui sandali feticci di ogni tipo umide corde vocali che svengono dopo l'acuto mentre discende il mistero carnale dall'empireo unghie di lacca dei bei piedi oh Wanda Osiris fuori tema è lo sguardo del viaggiatore che tira in mezzo cose con un'occhiata mentre il noto non smette di chiamare si vede qualcosa da un buco nel muro? cosa comporta in pratica $x+y = 1 = x+y-1 = 0$? cosa succede per esempio in Via Vigevano? con gli scuri accostati occhi obliqui dei sessi mostra il martirio il suo lato celeste ma niente accade per gradi secondo i principi del continuo ma con balzi giganteschi a totale rischio e pericolo.

2.2

off the cuff someone gives compliments to weeds and rubble that wreck the hierarchical system, but who complains about the countless ones? dusty blackberry bushes put fleas in your ear there's an osteria in Lacchiarella where they make chickpeas with pork rinds where you can find a small rhyme something with *lima* with *stima* with *prima* and best regards.*

it's the end that triggers the rhetoric and the beautiful epilogue of the outskirts the pathetic style oh *urbs pulcherrima* that raises (pardon!) its peroration of facades like at the end in Lorenteggio balconies that overlook well-watered meadows – you centers that luckily were never found! because of missing truth! here furious beauties wander with low-waist jeans girls and mopeds go about a sweet and evil hour arrives in the decay of the I – afternoons at the movies and immature breasts boots with laces flounder about darkening the windows of the little cars oh secret tabernacle ladder to god! while the being shows its lining of silk.

facts come to conduct business thank goodness the centuries have left labyrinths facing the sea thank goodness there's Genoa in extremis with the madonnas in the niches of the walls the cupolas that swell when the sun begins to set in the chaos of the golden fleece heavy butterflies raise and lower wings of mucus if you calculate hours and minutes 98% is made up of waiting oh the simple sea! which is complex without showing it! mind that kills its gems to remove the offenses!

dizziness that hovers over your sandals fetishes of every type sticky vocal cords that faint after high notes while the carnal mysteries descend from the empyrean polished nails of beautiful toes oh Wanda Osiris – off the subject is the gaze of the traveler who brings up things with a glance while the known does not stop calling can something be seen from a hole in the wall? what does $x+y = 1 = x+y-1 = 0$ involve in practice? what happens for example in Via Vigevano with the shadows brought together oblique eyes of the sexes the martyr shows his celestial side but nothing happens by degrees according to the principles of continuity but with gigantic leaps at full risk and danger.

---

* Translator's note: the poet here uses four words that are unrelated but that rhyme in Italian: *rima* [rhyme], *lima* [file], *stima* [esteem], *prima* [first].

la finta partenza e le molte ascese che si consumano ma dedalo che inventò il sorriso delle statue imbarazzante è finire in astratto per mancanza di mezzi tra la testa e il sesso almeno non siano ostili i cancelletti per degne dimore - giardini dell'assenza - oh nulla vilipeso! amico mio! - arriva prima dell'acqua punita in putredine prima delle piaghe da decubito - infermiere con le cosce sane - torni violentemente l'onore il profilo autentico il naso affilato una cosa abbandonata dal male le neve senza macchie sui davanzali dell' ospedale.

cosa ti auguro? ti auguro il tuo splendore calcareo alto sull'inguine e il buio dibattere - estasi secca che entusiasma i cereali - madre amorosa che si è tolta il grembiule - ti accompagni nel cammino polare ti mostri il versante nord di ogni cosa! meu frè, fossimo non solo intrecciando le dita fratelli – Sorella Madonna ci faccia dormire sotto un solo mantello.

the fake departure and the many ascents that wear themselves out but daedalus who invented the statues' smile it's awkward to end in abstraction for lack of means between the head and the sex may the gates of worthy dwellings at least not be hostile – gardens of absence – oh nothing reviled! my friend! – coming before the water punished in putrefaction before the plague of the bedsore – nurses with healthy thighs – may the honor the authentic profile the sharp nose a thing abandoned by evil the unspotted snow on the hospital's windowsills violently return.

what do I wish for you? I wish for your calcareous splendor high in your groin and the darkness to debate – dry ecstasy that thrills the grains – loving mother who took off her apron – may she accompany you in your polar journey may she show you the north face of everything! Brother, if only we were not just intertwining our brotherly fingers – Sister Madonna make us sleep under a single cloak.

3. sei facce di un cubo*

1.
scappa di corsa mandria di cose
groppe di bisonti invano
corrono impronte
dubitano silenziosi relitti
promesse dei sette cieli

2.
manca la parete verso strada
il muro di fondo è color pisello
uno scolapasta è ancora appeso
finito è il cubo delle delizie
la salvezza del quarto lato

3.
nessuno pensa
alle buone intenzioni dell'amo
alla concordia
con la bocca del pesce
ombra d'argento nell'acqua
naviga la trota primitiva
nubile senso di nessuno
con la scusa d'esser viva

---

* Le sei poesie sono state riprodotte su di una faccia di sei cubi, realizzati da Pietro Bologna nell'ambito di una interpretazione fotografica dello stile dorico ed esposti alla Galleria Lorenzo Vatalaro, ottobre 2018, Milano.

3. six faces of a cube*

1.
it takes off running herd of things
shoulders of bison vainly
running imprints
silent wrecks doubt
promises of seven heavens

2.
the wall toward the road is missing
the wall at the back is pea-colored
a colander is hanging still
finished is the cube of delights
the salvation of the fourth side

3.
no one thinks
of the hook's good intentions
about its harmony
with the mouth of the fish
silver shadow in the water
the primitive trout navigates
no one's unmarried feeling
with the excuse of being alive

---

* Each of these six poems was reproduced on one face of six cubes, created by Pietro Bologna in the context of a photographic interpretation of Doric style and displayed at Galleria Lorenzo Vatalaro, October 2018, Milan.

4.
stringere dilatare le pupille
fintanto che il cielo sarà viola
allora apparirà lo zafferano
sotto pressione è la verità
giurano il falso pie figure
palpebre si chiusero
e avvenne un'altra cosa
l'acqua scomparve
per amore della sete

5.
in una scatola da scarpe
ci sono cartoline e foto in posa
ridotto ad esistere sta zitto
incredibile apparire
è l'ora di chiedere perdono
disunione che più ama
ombra che si allunga
nostra deposizione

6.
sempre si ritrae
il contatto che si oscura
vicinanza a brandelli
più amata figura
sempre ricomposta
dall'istante che fu vista
punto per punto
come da vicino
forcine di tartaruga
buco dell'orecchino
lunghi giri fa l'amore
intatto il suo cuscino

4.
clenching enlarging the pupils
until the sky is purple
then it will seem saffron
under pressure it's the truth
pious figures swear it's false
eyelids close
and something else happens
the water disappears
through love of thirst

5.
in a shoebox
there are postcards and posed photos
reduced to existing it stays quiet
incredible to appear
it's the hour of asking forgiveness
disunion that loves more
shadow that lengthens
our deposition

6.
it always draws back
the contact that darkens
nearness to shreds
more beloved figure
always reassembled
from the moment it was seen
point by point
like from close up
tortoise-shell hairpins
earring holes
long walks making love
its pillow intact

4. vocalises

4.1
[(per non essere l'acqua che amo
   sarò dunque il suo ciottolo?)   (ondine gentili
                                                                sempre già lontane)]

  [(non vinca la trasparenza
    dove né tu né io
    ci potremmo vedere)]
  (ciottoli
    non sia durezza in voi
    levigati)
  (voi frutto del metodo
    esilio che ci risposa)]

[(non quadrato - ma
  rombo - che meglio interroga)
 (andantino con sentimento
  mancata rima)]

[(fialette di sole
 porta l'inverno)
 (disciplina
  che piange il suo sapere)
 (tornassi - le ho detto
  a dividere esseri vivi)]

[(vento magro - che non cerca l'arrivo)
  (né adagio né in fretta - punta di matita)
  (non muovere lo sfondo - mentre fai le righe)]

[(di spalle - più gentile saluto
  sagoma per poco - perdono di ogni luogo)]

4. vocalises

4.1
[(for not being the water that I love
  will I then be its pebble?)   (gentle waves
                                               ever farther away)]

[(the transparency may not win
  where neither you nor I
  will be able to see each other)]
[(pebbles
  may there not be hardness within you
  smoothed)
 (you fruit of the method
  exile that marries us again)]

[(not a square – but
 a rhombus – which asks better)
 (*andantino* with feeling
   lacking rhyme)]

[(winter brings
   little vials of sun)
 (discipline
   shouting its knowledge)
 (may you return – I told it
   to divide living beings)]

[(weak wind – not seeking arrival)
 (not slowly or in haste – pencil point)
 (don't move the background – while drawing the lines)]

[(behind you – kinder greeting
   nearly an outline – forgiveness of every place)]

4.2
[(libero dai sedotti - l'amore)

                              (fragili ore - anima
                                 che si deve bastare)
                              (accesa fiammella
                                 ardente verso il gelo)
                              (quand'anche perdita
                                 vuoto su misura)]

[(insorgono
   madri che chiamano in vita)
(istante glorioso
   già imitato di frodo)
(salta! ha detto l'attimo
   che conosce il fatto suo)]

[(figurata idea - solida figura)
(vedovo sapere
 rettilineo del mio lontano)
(trotterella il niente - accanto alla sua cosa
 la notte sta nelle sue braccia
 in posizione di sposa)]

4.2
[(free of the seduced – love)

                              (fragile hours – soul
                                that must be enough)
                              (a flame alight
                                that burns toward the chill)
                              (when lost as well
                                a custom-made void)]

[(they rise
  mothers who call to life)
 (glorious moment
  now poached imitated)
 (jump! said the moment
  that knows its business)]

[(illustrated idea – solid figure)
 (widowed knowledge
  straight from my distance)
 (nothingness trots – beside its thing
  that's in its arms at night
  in place of a bride)]

4.3
[(vecchi muri con nuovi geroglifici
   un graffio indica la pista - un'altra fontanella potabile)]

[(aumenta qualcosa insistendo anche sul niente
   se uno da Via Nirone arriva a Santa Marta
   e non incontra anima viva?)]

[oh
 (i zampeggianti ondulanti bovi - come traduce Emilio Villa!)
 (quel complicato profumo sono vacche da latte
   da via Torino sempre dritto verso sud
   fino alle fruscianti - voi rogge padane)]

[(clandestini! - candidati a fare poemi)
  (anime esterne - versi con un piede alzato)
  (scuote la groppa - bufalo dei vostri polmoni
   poesia - vuoto di un tamburo)]

[(e i sassi bianchi del Monte Ventoso?)
  (in ordine d'arrivo: Francesco Petrarca 1336
   luglio 2000 Marco Pantani - con il vento contro)]

[(deludono le cose? - finché non saranno trasparenti
   e la trasparenza più niente?
  (in pratica: andate al sodo - dopo il corpo viene il bello!)
  (illic a corporeis ad incorporea volucri cogitatione transiliens)
  (bambini occidentali
    che infatti in quel passaggio trasalite - lacrime di piccoli padroni)]

[(e i sassi? la loro siccità? le disperate imitazioni?)]

[(chi continua a trattare la mancanza come un credito?)]

[(cambia colore un filo nel tappeto persiano?
    si appella un colore a un altro colore?
    si accoppia davanti alle signore?
    è stato fedele?
    ha conservato la vita interiore
    l'ira primordiale il primo amore?)]

4.3

[(old walls with new hieroglyphics
  a scratch points the way – another safe drinking fountain)]

[(does something increase also insisting on nothing
  if someone from Via Nirone arrives at Santa Marta
  and doesn't meet a living soul?)]

[oh
  (the thundering undulating oxen – as Emilio Villa translates!)
  (that complicated scent they are milk cows
   from Via Torino straight ahead toward the south
   to the rustling – you irrigation ditches of the Po Valley)]

[(stowaways! – nominated to write poems)
  (external souls – verses with one foot raised)
  (shake their rumps – buffalo of your lungs
   poetry – hollow of a drum)]

[(and the white stones of Monte Ventoso?)
  (in order of arrival: Francesco Petrarca 1336
   July 2000 Marco Pantani – against the wind)]

[(do things disappoint? – until they're transparent
   and the transparency more nothing?
  (in practice: get to the point – the best comes after the body!)
  (*illic a corporeis ad incorporea volucri cogitatione transiliens*)
  (western children
   who in fact in that passage jump – tears of little masters)]

[(and the stones? their dryness? the desperate imitations?)]

[(who still treats absence like a credit?)]

[(does a thread in the Persian rug change color?
  does one color appeal to another color?
  does one copulate in front of the ladies?
  was he faithful?
  did the first love preserve
  its inner life its primordial rage?)]

[(è questo che fa vibrare l'insieme
che si agita come tortura di gioia
che piace così tanto alla gente
come al suo culmine - il linguaggio tremante?)]

[(is this what makes the whole vibrate
that tosses about like torture of joy
that people like so much
as if at its peak – the trembling language?)]

seelenboulevard / seelenboulevard
(1999)

1. come quando

come quando se fosse metropoli conurbato l'individuo pieno di folla sia dentro che fuori cosa comporta l'origine persistente come una piccola mosca? minutissima infanzia e strana bellezza del gelo nell'anestesia della mente cade un volo di foglie su di te in una scatola da scarpe sono rimaste le foto in bianco e nero da qualche parte c'è un vecchio intonaco e ombre di verderame qualcuno piantò la vite contro il muro in un giorno positivo? come nuvola di moscerini insorgono brevemente i minuti degli umili e fanno flop per la seconda volta adieu! mentre nel cielo passa un enorme dirigibile come un plusvalore fantastico un'idea volante sul tuo buco dell'origine che intona we are the champions?

cosa succede ai cortei tipo Pellizza da Volpedo? vengono verso di noi frontalmente - quelli davanti con il cappello sono i padri - e noi? cosa ci facciamo tra palazzo Malaspina e l'uomo con la camicia bianca? ho gridato: ancora un minuto per guardarvi e sarò con voi - come nel quadro andremo verso nessuno ora che il grande lontano è finito - smantellato in ogni luogo - qualcuno ti ha visto su un treno per Voghera - guardavi fuori dal finestrino insanabili particolari - i gloriosi inconoscibili conosciuti tale quali.

accessori e lontane delizie come la zucca che si avvinghia poi molla la presa in autunno - in giro c'è un effetto d'anima - crusca lucente di un vespero strano - è l'inespresso che manda ambasciatori? indovina! point sublime e magnifici ingombri! di ciò vi dovete accontentare come di ossessioni irripetibili - a queste condizioni sia il corpo il nostro torbido riparo - opaco conoscere che assolve la sua mente.

come coppo sul tetto come tegola su tegola come il due con l'uno che lo interna tanto vale il dono dei miopi da vicino mistico vapore il sole che affonda come un biscotto nel latte oh maschera della carità - amore ospedaliere che vuole strafare con zuppiere della festa come dare un carnale forfait come un viaggio perfetto con il mare sempre a sinistra ora che tutto fa parte dell'arrivo nessun posto è sbagliato - distrazione che aleggia leggera leggera intorno al chiodo fisso?

qualcosa annuncia un mancante? o si annuncia da solo in purezza - teorico crac - misere leggi di fronte alla varietà del delitto - l'uguale è il vero labirinto? che

1. like when

like when if he were a metropolis the conurbated individual full of a crowd both inside and out what does the origin involve persistent like a small fly? smallest childhood and strange beauty of the frost in the anesthesia of the mind a flight of leaves falls upon you the photos in black and white were left in a shoebox somewhere there's old plaster and verdigris shadows did someone plant the vines against the wall on a favorable day? like a cloud of gnats the minutes of the humble rise briefly and flop for the second time adieu! while in the sky an enormous dirigible passes like a fantastic added-value a flying idea about your hole of the beginning that starts to sing *we are the champions*?

what happens at the processions like Pellizza da Volpedo? they come directly toward us – the ones in front with the hats are the fathers – and we? what are we doing between Palazzo Malaspina and the man with the white shirt? I shouted: another minute of watching and I'll be with you – like in the painting we will go toward no one now that the great far away is over – every place dismantled – someone saw you on a train to Voghera – you were looking out the window relentless details – the glorious unknowables known as such.

accessories and distant delights like the pumpkin that winds itself then loosens its hold in the fall – there's an effect of the soul going around – shining bran of a strange late afternoon – is it the unexpressed that sends ambassadors? guess! *point sublime* and magnificent impediments! you will have to content yourselves with that as with unrepeatable obsessions – may our cloudy refuge be the body to these conditions – opaque knowledge that absolves its mind.

like pantile on the roof like tile upon tile like the second that envelops the first like the gift of the short-sighted up close mystical vapor the sun that sinks into like a cookie in milk oh mask of charity – hospital love that wants to overdo with holiday soup tureens like giving a carnal flat rate like a perfect trip with the sea always on your left now that everything is part of the arrival no place is wrong – distraction that hovers ever so lightly around her obsession?

does something announce an absence? or is it announced on its own in purity? – theoretical crash – poor laws in the face of the variety of crime – is the real

frappose la porta aperta per il vuoto reciproco? il fatto ha preso posto e non si vede nient'altro - oh annunciate e addolorate - corpo che si nasconde nel vestito - cosce calde d'inverno e fresche d'estate - segreti esplosivi - una sorpresa una resa - forse un indizio che aiuta - oh già vedova attesa!

credere è contro commerciare? (alette di merluzzo in carta di giornale) - ti avrei detto: non finire mai con l'uguale - non chiedere al bene di arrivare puntuale - e il bluff della moneta? l'ortofrutta in genere? koyft zhe koyft zhe papirosn! tutto quello che avanza è anima - come dire una celeste discarica? i tic dello spirito il suo deserto tattile? oh privazione che sconfessa tutte le misure - oh inverno bambino che contiene cose rare!

labyrinth the same? putting an open door between the reciprocal void? while the fact has taken its place and nothing else can be seen? – oh women! heralded and saddened – body that hides in its clothes – warm thighs of winter and cool ones of summer – explosive secrets – a surprise a surrender – maybe a clue that helps – oh long-widowed wait!

is believing against dealing? (codfish fins in newspaper) – I would have told you: never end with an equal sign – don't ask the good to arrive on time – and the sham of the coin? fruits and vegetables in general? *koyft zhe koyft zhe papirosn!* everything that's left over is soul – how do you say a heavenly dump? the tics of the sprit its tactile desert? oh privation that rejects all measures – oh child winter that contains rare things!

2. barbara celarent

tutto l'ordine cronologico va rifatto di sana pianta anche la nascita che ebbe presentimenti di ogni genere basta saltare un passaggio e tutto diventa introvabile le parole in fila erano tutte figure solide come un covo d'essere come un coniglio d'angora?

fin dove arriva l'ampiezza di questo stare dove si estende l'io e il suo punto dolente sotto il cielo che rinfaccia universali? - e se fosse da provare con la pazza gioia? o la sonnolenza anestetica che spianta il duplice tra te e qualcosa lo spegnimento di quell'incandescenza il continuo emendamento di una cosa?

sanatorie e maddalene invalidata ragione - provvidenze dell'altissimo anche acquisite in solido - profumi di violette e rococò - e la saggia scala del dissimile? e i sistemi estesi fatti di particole? immagina di aprire la finestra sul fiume Huang Ho: quante sostituzioni allontanano la morte? astuzie dell'amore rimescolate solitudini - che fioriscono come balconi dirimpetto - moderata è la verità - un po' meno come al solito - ma niente si può chiudere se non può anche continuare - l'istante ha fatto marameo - gira la ruota dei sorteggi - ottenessi almeno l'appoggio dell'invano.

come preparare l'io al suo dissimile? come offrire al nulla un buon motivo come la cura di quei minimi quando si presenta l'astratto in forma umana? allora ci fu la festa del saltellare come i grilli in una notte canterina che va lontano come lontano è restare?

presa alla sprovvista gattina in una scatola di cartone - trasportata in posti lontani poesia allo stato puro - sibilano fruste su parole attardate - tovaglie ingombre sere sfortunate cedono le ginocchia mentre ricerchi un diversivo?

come fatta notte in croci e in letti in reliquati corpi brevi morfine giubilo di seni lotte vere in piacere assunte benvenuti nel pensiero che ti spreme come un tubo di conserva sfrontata coppia che fa il vero con un fatto adesso che il sopruso si veste dalla festa animata vagina - sua eccentrica risposta?

2. barbara celarent

the whole chronological order must be completely redone even the birth that had premonitions of every sort it's enough to skip a transition and everything becomes impossible to find were all the words in a row solid figures like a hideout of being like an angora rabbit?

where is it going the breadth of this staying where the *I* spreads and its sore spot beneath the heaven that remakes universals – and if it were to be proven with crazy joy? or the anesthetic sleepiness that roots out the double between you and something the extinguishing of that incandescence the continuous emendation of something?

amnesties and Magdalenes denied reason – providential events of the highest also truly acquired – scents of violets and rococo – and the wise scale of the dissimilar? and the extended systems made of particles? imagine opening the window onto the Huang Ho: how many substitutions distance death? tricks of love shuffled solitudes – that flourish like facing balconies – the truth is moderated – a little less as is its custom – but nothing can be closed if it cannot also continue – the moment thumbed its nose – the wheel of fortune turns – may it at least obtain the support of what's in vain.

how do you prepare the *I* for its dissimilar? how do you offer to nothing a good reason like the care of those minimums when the abstract presents itself in human form? was there then the festival of leaping like crickets in a chirping night that goes far like far is remaining?

kitten caught unaware in a carboard box – transported to distant places poetry in its pure state – whips hiss on lingering words – cluttered tablecloths unfortunate evening do the knees give in while you're looking for relief?

like night spent on crosses and in beds in relic bodies brief morphines rejoicing of breasts true struggles disguised as pleasure welcomes in thought that squeezes you like a tube preserves the shameless couple that makes truth with one fact now that the abuse is dressed for the party animated vagina – its eccentric response?

l'abile grammatico spinge le cose verso il finale si scinde lo zolfo il verderame tentano la sorte che li fa puri per questo i verbi alzano altari altre volte si svenano da soli?

a tu per tu ti avrei consigliato di precedermi con l'oblio volontario - oh il ritorno segreto dei numeri che ogni volta si salutano - ti avrei detto: mi lancio da uno fino a cento per risentire quell'uno tante volte - mentendo ti ho detto di salvare l'attesa come l'anellino al tuo dito - ti ho detto che i conti che non tornano vanno all'infinito.

minore è la divisione da grandi distanze - linee ondulate per fare le colline - le greche sui vasi che significano: ecco cosa sono in breve le onde del mare! oh stile dell'anima disegni dei bambini! - ma che dire dei bigodini del sabato? della buona salute e delle scarpe comode? - nell'insieme non risultano ammanchi - ma niente è compiuto se ci sono in giro i viventi - (che riaprono i casi che scrivono lettere ai morti) - (ehi bello mio!) che pensavi a un inizio da capogiro - dal predellino della corriera spuntò la sua scarpina - era il millenovecentocinquanta - (più eri maschio - più pregavi di essere bambina).

the able grammarian pushes things toward the conclusion the sulfur the verdigris is broken up they tempt the fate that makes them pure is this why the verbs erect altars at other times slashing their wrists by themselves?

face to face I would have advised you to precede me with voluntary oblivion – oh the secret return of the numbers that greet each other every time – I would have said: I dashed from one to a hundred to hear that one again so many times – lying I told you to save the waiting like the little ring on your finger – I told you that the counts don't return they go to infinity.

the division is less from great distances – wavy lines in order to do the hills – the stripes on the pots that signify: that's all they are in short the waves of the sea! oh style of the soul children's drawings! – but what do you say about Saturday's curlers? about good health and comfortable shoes? – on the whole shortages don't result – but nothing is completed if the living are around – (who reopen matters who write letters to the dead) – (hey my friend!) what did you think of a dizzying beginning – from the footboard of the coach her pump stuck out – it was 1950 – (the more you were a man – the more you asked to be a little girl).

3. sasso piatto

facente funzione fino a quando caduto da cavallo anche il soggetto all'inizio è un volo ogni caduta nel sottosopra dei sensi sembrano pesciolini intenzioni argentee acciughine nel mare e voilà: in ghingheri uscì di casa l'essere brilla mentre passa di mano oscuri cherubini difendono l'entrata si sfiorano capezzoli nella folla del tram luoghi pubblici adescano i più soli l'economia tiene tutti a distanza tombola! per acclamazione e per intero vuoto compreso laddove penetrò cadono perle e rugiade di bijoux il fatto fu stordito attribuito a più soggetti ne gode l'essere che riprese tutto nel suo seno ricco di cose perse c'è un tempo di fortuna doglie di gioia in nuvole nere naviga verso di sé chi invece si allontana.

l'amplesso che molto condonò anche l'istante è rimasto di stucco la grazia è spaesata tra soggetti vacanti guarda davvero dal comò una graziosa civetta? quando l'amore aggredì e divelse l'insieme scuro mantice di esseri vivi - oh palpebra amore! perché piangendo sbattono candide ali liberate cicogne - liberazione senza fine con puri battiti intonando mille gioie?

non è il lontano che manca a partire da subito aggiungi ai residenti tutti quelli di passaggio - e i sedotti? che ascendono con anime e mongolfiere al tramonto? che aprono le braccia e sembrano più del doppio? - e i negativi dei fotografi? i particolari che fanno riflettere - il suo pube bianco come un pensiero fanatico? figure a colori! ex voto dei santuari voi intere per miracolo! perché tra i pullman delle gite scolastiche cerco ancora quella grazia invulnerabile? il suo polso fine con il polsino abbottonato il braccialettino infantile l'alleanza infrangibile la nostra promessa a perdifiato?

nessun viaggio può farti trovare il picchio che stava davanti alla finestra né quel giro sintetico che passa sui vuoti con un saltello anche il nulla va bene fin che è piccolo non più grande di un respiro o fosse quello potente del mare! nella lunga notte l'andare e venire l'anima che si alza e si abbassa mette sul gas la caffettiera attacca il ferro da stiro prova il vestito da ballo senza l'intenzione di uscire.

3. flat stone

acting until fallen from the horse also the subject at the beginning is a flight every fall in the confusion of the senses seems like minnows silvery intentions silverfish in the sea and voilà: dressed up he left home the being shines while it passes through the hand dark cherubs defend the entrance they graze nipples in the crowd on the tram public places they lure those most alone the economy holds everyone at a distance bingo! through acclamation and entirely gaps included where he penetrated pearls and dewdrops of jewels fall the action was stunned attributed to many subjects it enjoys its being that took up everything in its breast rich in lost things there's a time of fortune pangs of joy in black clouds he navigates toward himself from some instead he moves away.

the embrace that forgave so much even the current moment was stunned among vacant subjects and disoriented grace is that really a pretty little owl on the dresser? when love attacked and uprooted the whole, the dark bellows of living beings – oh eyelid love! why do pale wings of freed storks flap crying – continuous liberation with pure beats singing a thousand joys?

it is not the distant that is missing starting from immediately you add to the residents all those in transit – and the seduced? who ascend with souls and hot air balloons at sunset? who open their arms and seem more than double? – and the photographers' negatives? the details that strike you – her pubis blank like a fanatical thought? figures in color! votives of the sanctuaries all of you whole by a miracle! why among the buses of the school trips do I still seek that invulnerable grace? her thin wrist with the cuff buttoned the small childish bracelet the unbreakable alliance our promise at the top of our voices?

no journey can make you find the tapping there was by the window nor that brief trip that passes through the voids with a leap even nothingness is OK as long as it's small no larger than a breath or if it were the powerful one of the sea! in the long night the coming and going the soul that rises and descends puts the coffeemaker on the gas plugs in the iron tries on the ball gown with no intention of going out.

a prima vista non manca niente dall'insieme nemmeno il mio mancante oh zattera di un piccolo minuto nuvoletta della cipria perché non facciamo un duetto? io faccio l'intervallo mentre tu esulti sui tuoi tacchi? oh equità del complesso - oh fessura del tuo vivere scintillante pupilla - per i primi tempi in quest'inverno - ti prego - sia assolta la mente che per scaldarsi saltella.

l'espressione - ti ho visto più di una volta - era un sasso piatto da far rimbalzare sull'acqua urrah! mio lontano - detta e ridetta mia figura! invece disse: il mio male che non basta! cade il sasso come a scuola quando faceva scena muta - come una gioia che è vera senza prova? ancora un minuto sia concesso a quel bambino - mentre il boia è distratto da un uccellino.

come blindata nei suoi cembali orchestrina con ritornello che usa l'abbandono come un rimedio - tra prendere e lasciare subire è più grande del fare? o è tal quale? anche interrompere l'uguale con l'uguale o il simile con la faccia da furbo che ripassa due volte all'incasso? - ma che dire delle divisioni che fanno numero? e Tarzan che usa la liana come la logica - come la poesia l'ineffabile? oh slanci avventati - esseri su misura che fanno moltitudine - e il verso bello? - giostra della nostra privazione - pensiero fuori tiro - sotto il dito puntato di dio?

at first glance nothing is missing from the whole not even my missing oh raft of small minute little cloud of powder why don't we do a duet? I'll do the intermission while you exult in your heels? oh evenness of the whole – oh split in your living sparkling pupil – for the first time this winter – I beg you – may the mind be absolved that throbs from burning itself.

the expression – I saw you more than once – it was a flat stone for skipping over the water hurrah! my distance – my figure said over and over! rather it said: my ache which is not enough! does the stone fall like at school when doing a silent scene – like a joy that is true without proof? may that child be allowed another minute – while the executioner is distracted by a little bird.

as if armored by its small orchestra cymbals with a refrain that uses abandonment as a cure – between taking and leaving is suffering more than doing? or is it the same? and to interrupt one thing with the same or its similar with the sneaky face of one who passes twice through the turnstile? – but what is there to say about the divisions that make up the numbers? and Tarzan who uses the vine like logic – like poetry uses the ineffable? oh reckless dash – custom-made beings that make up the multitude – and the beautiful verse? – merry-go-round of our hardship – thought out of range – under the pointing finger of god?

4. silent

svelato dal non accaduto - ne sanno qualcosa
gli scricchiolii di notte
i mobili che assistono ai fatti

belle ginocchia - felici con la gonna
inconsapevoli
se devi piangere non metterti l'ombretto

non vanno dall'altra parte
parole - ma verso di noi
fin che non saremo abbattuti

un passo prima del traguardo chi onora la storia del nostro attendere mentre irrompe la nascita su madri e neonati? la chiameremo festa del filo di lana questo istante insuperabile che con spavento spalanca gli occhi belli?

lo sai tu perché il senso si accumula sui confini come chi vuole migrare ahi rondinelle! o diventare un fatto o un facsimile con gli occhiali scuri come se avesse bisogno di svignarsela?

per questo non ti ho trovato in generale né in quella luce caotica tra nuvole nere quando gridai a te che di spalle non sentivi: perché sei andata nel visto invece di vedere?

e quel chicco d'essere? solo se ti spaventassi è utile il contesto e il suo sproloquio non vedi che è un finto finale un finalino come la scossa di piacere in ore smorte quando sapere è come ricambiare?

e i fortunati espedienti che ci lasciano vivi? la trasparenza confusa con torbidi ripari? oh il ritorno dei trasfigurati! creaturina deforme fu l'errore - motivo per cui torna indietro l'amore?

e lo scricciolo della neve? se l'hai visto è la tua nostalgia - o è bastato pronunciarlo alla lavagna - parola che prima lo dice poi fa la spia?

4. silent

        revealed by what didn't happen – they know something about it
        the creaking at night
        the furniture that witnesses the events

        beautiful knees – work well with the skirt
        unaware
        if you have to cry don't put on eye shadow

        they don't go to the other side
        words – but toward us
        until we're knocked down

one step before the finish line who honors the history of our waiting while birth bursts over mothers and newborns? shall we call it the festival of the woolen thread this incomparable minute that opens wide with fright the beautiful eyes?

you know why feeling accumulates at the borders like someone who wants to migrate ouch the swallows! or wants to become a fact or a facsimile with dark glasses as if there were need to slink away?

this is why I didn't find you in general or in that chaotic light among black clouds when I shouted to you who could not hear me behind: why did you come into view instead of seeing?

and that grain of being? only if you were frightened is the context useful and its ranting don't you see that it's a false ending a tailpiece like the shock of pleasure in dull hours when knowing is like returning a favor?

and the lucky expedients that leave us alive? the confused transparency with cloudy lenses? oh the return of the transfigured! a little deformed infant was our error – the reason why love turned back?

and the creaking of the snow? if you saw it it's your nostalgia – or was it enough to speak it to the blackboard – word that first you say and then it becomes an informer?

sogno che intorbida l'uovo attimi aggiuntivi rondoni che sorvolano i tetti scommesse vinte senza muovere un dito il mancante ha i suoi astuti misurini oh varietà del vedere! in povertà stiamo seduti su un gradino tu mi dici: bastava un niente di tutto il niente che avevi.

con i tacchi tra le rotaie del tram bellezza in lacrime incalzata da ordini e contrordini se penso che i tuoi polpacci erano torsi di statue - oh impurità degli assenti! preparare il futuro è come averlo come preparare la salsa per l'inverno Anna che fa passare il riso con le unghie - che becchettano come veloci uccellini - ma di notte! cosa fanno i vestiti molli sui loro appendini?

vecchi pavimenti tirati con la cera mamme innocenti si guardano allo specchio aspettano la colpa in un oscuro regalo - c'è un cratere di farina e i rossi dell'uovo si asciugano lacrime con le mani infarinate ridono da sole con le facce dipinte scoprono il trucco che libera dal male.

tempo di compassione lingua cruciale - non tu almeno - non sfigurarci mentre ci rammemori - mostri l'improprio le sue parti buone – quel poco che ci fece maceria - di cui bello era il cielo.

dream that clouds the egg additional moments swifts that fly over the roofs bets won without moving a finger the missing one has its clever measuring cups oh varieties of seeing! we are seated on a step in poverty you tell me: one nothing out of all the nothing you had would be enough.

with her heels between the tram tracks beauty in tears pursued by orders and counter-orders if I think that your calves were torsos of statues – oh impurity of the absent! preparing the future is like having it like preparing the sauce for winter Anna who sifts through the rice with her fingernails – that peck away like quick little birds – but at night! what do the soft clothes do on their hangers?

old waxed floors innocent mamas look at themselves in the mirror expecting blame in a dark gift – there's a crater of flour and egg yolks tears are dried with their floured hands they laugh by themselves with their painted faces they discover the makeup that frees them from pain.

time of compassion crucial language – at least not you – don't distort us while you remember us – show the improper its good parts – the bit that made us rubble – whose beauty was the sky.

bambina teoria / child theory
(1990)

1. un moccioso chiede di te

infanzia dei tuoi sensi
bambino piccolo
conosco il tuo chiamare
gridolini di disordine
scompiglio per spaiare
cosa da cosa
passerotti dalla mamma
per vederli volare
non ti ricorda qualcosa?
una scena spettacolare?
lontano e luminoso
un abbandono
lacrime saporite
buone da leccare?

note.
1 – Basta con le cose dolci - caramelle dell'infanzia da mettere in tasca per dopo - bambina che davanti a te ho scoperto solitudine - meglio di niente è rovesciarsi sulla riva come il mare - obbligata felicità come davanti a nessuno - mente oceano - onda che da sempre gode ricadere.
2 – Dimora non sia - luogo insistente - se osservi anche le foglie si alternano con la luce finemente intessuta di ombre e penombre che alla fine si depongono come scialli a uncinetto sul suolo nudo come su nude spalle carnali chiarori - sono transiti perfetti i nostri incontri inanellati come volubili lasciti per chi? mentre vagano polveri di memoria dove un solo particolare comanda.
3 – Se senti la ghiandaia che insorge contro il proprio grido quello è l'apice dell'espressione l'aridità delle spighe che chiedono più sete nomadi dell'umano è l'ora di non insistere mentre il divenire macina chilometri ancora una volta l'unico è sventato in questa sera nostrana tutti compiangono il loro amore messo in salvo il suo ultimo squillo che si allontana.

1. a brat asks for you

childhood of your feelings
small child
I recognize your call
little shouts of disarray
commotion to separate
thing from thing
fledgling sparrows from their mother
in order to see them fly
don't you remember something?
a spectacular scene?
distant and bright
an abandonment
tasty tears
good for licking?

notes.
1 — Enough with sweet things – childhood candies to put in your pocket for later – little girl who in front of you I discovered solitude – falling down on the shore like the sea is better than nothing – obligatory happiness as if in front of no one – ocean mind – wave that has always liked falling.
2 — It may not be a dwelling – persistent place – if you also observed the leaves alternating with the light finely woven of shadows and glimmering powders that in the end deposit themselves like crocheted shawls on the bare ground as if on bare carnally glimmering shoulders – they are perfect transits our encounters strung together like unstable legacies for whom? while dusts of memory wander where a single detail commands.
3 — If you hear the jay that rises against its own cry which is the apex of expression the aridity of the ears that ask for more thirst nomads of the human it's the hour of not insisting while the becoming grinds kilometers once again the unique is averted in this evening of ours everyone is sorry for their saved love its final ringing that's moving away.

apparente futuro
gonna a pieghe
chiama l'origine
nero pube di aprile
implora distinzione
la mente madreperla
chicco dopo chicco
coroncina del rosario
palme galoppanti
nel tuo vento scuro
barbariche ciglia
fino dove mi assomiglio.

4 – Sempre è decadere il bello di qualcosa mentre tutto è respiro - se dai retta è per mettersi in pari - mancanti da molti luoghi solcano i mari veloci sardine le antenne che picchiano sono un promemoria ondeggiano barche da pesca nel vento intricato si oscurano gli specchi in stanze d'affitto feroce assomigliare femmina me che da sola mi fai fare corpo nudo in una pelliccia di castoro.
5 – Dove imperversa l'insieme in successione anche lenta molto si gioca sul contrario piccolo botto di un fiammifero s'infrange sul corpo il discorso diretto piaghe molli ha la notte di primavera mia folle dedizione che invoco io su di me potenza straniera.
6 – Un mistero è lo scambio dell'identico ma se io fossi la tua palpebra allora è come al cinema pupilla che lancia figure pensa alle righe tratteggiate in terza media le proiezioni che portano lontano fuori dal foglio da disegno come le cosce sotto la cattedra della maestra.

apparent future
pleated skirt
calls its origin
April's black pubis
begs for distinction
the mother-of-pearl mind
grain after grain
little crown of the rosary
galloping palms
in your dark wind
barbaric eyelashes
to the point where I look like myself.

4 — The beauty of something is always declining while everything is breath – if you pay attention it's for making yourself equal – missing from many places rapid sardines they ply the seas the thrashing masts are a reminder fishing boats rock in the heavy wind mirrors darken in rented rooms cruelly resembling oh woman me whom you leave alone to act a naked body in a beaver fur.
5 — Where the whole rages in succession even slowly much is played on the other hand little crack of a match direct discourse shatters on the body the spring night has soft wounds my mad devotion that I invoke foreign power upon myself.
6 — The exchange of identical is a mystery but if I were your eyelid then it's like at the cinema a pupil that throws figures think of the broken lines in middle school the projections that carry far beyond the drawing paper like the thighs beneath the teacher's desk.

senza commento
cosa sola
un moccioso chiede di te
io disabitato
(non è più lui - dicono
le vicine)
tocca a te lingua intercambiabile
tornare suoi tuoi passi
arrossire
davanti al fagottino abbandonato
che non sai cosa vuol dire.

7 – La rotazione del soggetto in senso orario prima o poi si ritrova in vista dell'inizio nel qual caso è la fine ma se uno non avesse più tempo tu pensi che allora andrebbe al sodo? no e poi no fino all'ultimo c'è un evento come una smorfia d'espressione come dire metti al posto di questo due mele o quel che capita metti in salvo l'elenco dei propositi monetine dei poveri senza proporzione.
8 – Potessimo parlare esclamare potessimo almeno parlare come sanguinare come lasciarsi dissanguare come se fosse possibile paragonare tutto in toto con intento spettacolare come sul monte Tabor senza lasciare sospetti per racconti di tipo popolare nemmeno la stringa delle scarpe sfuggita all'ascensione.
9 – Eppure sia onorato il luogo che tiene duro sotto la sua stellina che si accende in verticale sopra Via Col di Lana dove il tram picchia sullo scambio verso la rimessa di Via Custodi nell'ultima corsa serale ugualmente sia lodata la collina e quell'orchestrina di coperchi per il bollito misto alla piemontese nei giorni del santo patrono quando perfino le galline avranno il risotto giallo con lo zafferano.

without comment
just one thing
a brat asks about you
I, emptied out
(it's no longer him – say
the neighbors)
it's your turn interchangeable language
to turn back your steps
blush
in front of the abandoned little bundle
whose meaning you don't know.

7 — The clockwise rotation of the subject sooner or later finds itself in sight of the beginning in which case it's the end but if one does not have more time do you think that then it would get to the point? a thousand times no there's an event like a grimacing expression as if to say substitute for these two apples or whatever happens save the list of intentions small change of the poor out of proportion.
8 — If we could speak exclaim if we could at least speak like bleeding like letting yourself bleed out as if it were possible to compare everything in toto with spectacular intent like on Mount Tabor without leaving suspects for stories of the popular sort not even the laces of the shoes that avoided the ascent.
9 — And yet may the place be honored that holds strong under its little star that lights straight up over Via Col di Lana where the tram strikes on the transfer toward the garage in Via Custodi on the last evening run similarly may the hill be praised and that small orchestra of lids for the Piedmontese *bollito misto* on the days of the patron saint when even the chickens will have risotto yellow with saffron.

2. duo soledad

un suono d'argento zampillò
fu facile diventare quasi uguali
ma quando speravo che l'essere
fosse più grande di me
quando pensavo: per mal che vada
sarò la sua preghiera
bambino al primo giorno di scuola
appello con nome e cognome
per intero - per sempre due cose
bambino mezzo vero
ma profonda era la borsa della spesa
madri nel giorno di mercato
oh palme di Guadalampur
bollicine si staccano dal cuore
idrolitina che rende tutto esagerato
anche chiamare - o è subito
o diventa invocare.

in complesse formazioni - breve io
o tra ferro e azzurro come a Genova
lungo la notte - vento che scintilla
più insisti più diventa imperfetto
ciò che fu breve - mai sarà l'improvviso
oh lunghe esposizioni - giri completi
intorno al polo - Grande Orsa
vano è il tuo morire - così noi
continuativi come un debito
pronti a ribadire
metropoli è la lingua
come salire a Loreto
tu che stai a Ripamonti
palpebre a matita
gatta di pupille
adesso non porti più le calze
è primavera
manna dal cielo - i somiglianti
l'improprio che fa scintille.

2. duo soledad

a sound of silver spouted
it was easy to become almost equal
but when I hoped that the being
would be larger than me
when I thought: whatever evil may come
I will be its prayer
child on the first day of school
roll-call with first and last name
in full – two things forever
child half true
but deep was the shopping bag
mothers on market day
oh palms of Kuala Lumpur
bubbles break off from the heart
powder for sparkling water that makes everything exaggerated
even calling – it's either right away
or it becomes pleading.

in complex formations – *I* brief
or between iron and blue like in Genoa
through the night – wind that flashes
the more you insist the more it becomes imperfect
that which was short – will never be sudden
oh long exposures – complete circles
around the pole – Ursa Major
your dying is in vain – so we
ongoing like a debt
ready to confirm
metropolis is the language
like going up to Loreto
you who are at Ripamonti
penciled eyelids
cat of pupils
now you no longer wear stockings
it's spring
manna from heaven – the similarities
the improper that makes sparks fly.

mandrie e frasi - epopea
al galoppo - come fare man bassa
cadono dalla gioia - birilli
una garanzia è la folla
ogni vuoto è un invito
perché quando chiami
chi risponde ha sbagliato?
eccomi
tua vuota dimora
territoriale è l'essere
stanza di calce nuova
sventolò da lontano un'idea
ma era una gonna bianca - da vicino
e arrivò aprile urrah!
si confuse la linea
che volevo attraversare
le ho chiesto: non si vedono confini
come si fa per passare?

chi invece congiunse - invocò
oh malinconia del continuo
distanti esche - diminuiscono per primi
i paragoni - si procede soltanto per interi
(è pericoloso! accidenti) - invece
bello è assomigliare - per esempio
tirarla per le lunghe
con cose affini - stare in giro
ancora per cinque minuti
salutare toccando il Borsalino
(è il massimo)
per intanto apre e chiude
falde maliziose il cappotto nuovo
bianche ginocchia - per quest'inverno
un grazioso cappellino.

orfeo dell'io
come chi in un grembo
sia puro sentire
ma nati per discriminare
come discriminato è il sensibile
bambini degli anni cinquanta

herds and phrases – galloping
epic – how to do it easily
they fall with joy – bowling pins
the crowd is a guarantee
every void is an invitation
why when you call
whoever responding was wrong?
here I am
your empty dwelling
the being is territorial
newly whitewashed room
an idea waved from afar
but it was a white skirt – up close
and April came hurrah!
the line blurred
that I wanted to cross
I asked her: aren't boundaries seen
how does one get by?

who instead united – appealed to
oh continuous sadness
distant decoys – they lessened at first
the comparisons – one proceeds only by wholes
(it's dangerous! damn) – instead
beauty is resembling – for example
to pull it dragging on
with similar things – being around
for another five minutes
touching the Borsalino in greeting
(that's the most)
for the moment opening and closing
the mischievous layers of the new skirt
white knees – for this winter
a lovely small hat.

orpheus of the I
like someone in a lap
may feeling be pure
but born to differentiate
as the tangible requires
children of the 1950s

davanti al verderame azzurro
che non si può toccare
lo zolfo che fa lacrimare
oh sole dosato dell'inverno
parsimonia di questo cielo
solaio dove seccano fagioli
(sostiene il tramonto - in controluce
una nera figura)

suona la mente
con gli ultimi legnetti
appare una luce tardiva
l'acqua di torba
le fulve erbe dei puri.

in merito alle proporzioni
osserva dove il senso
sembra sonnecchiare
come d'inverno - tra stecchi aerei
piccoli gufi - sui paletti
delle vigne - i veloci scalpelli
di un picchio
colui che tiene i conti - lasci perdere
(è un consiglio da amico)
legge disattenta - sostituibile parola
ma tu
se dici oh
tieni bilanciato tutto da sola.

il tuo grembo e l'imbrunire
tuoni di stagnola
cima di noi - dove affondo
come il rosso e il nero
che si addice
luna sanguinaria - che scompiglia
la notte massiccia - lunga gonna
da zingara - divelta fede
ma quel levare di cupole
sollievo delle anime
sia una piuma il volere
clemenza del profondo

before the blue verdigris
that cannot be touched
the sulfur that makes you cry
oh rationed sun of winter
parsimony of this sky
attic where beans dry
(supporting the sunset – backlit
a black figure)

the mind sounds
with the last bits of wood
a late light appears
the peaty water
the tawny grasses of the pure.

with respect to the proportions
note where the sensation
seems to doze
like winter – among aerial sticks
little owls – on the poles
of the vines – the rapid drills
of a woodpecker
he who keeps count – let it go
(is a friend's advice)
careless law – replaceable word
but you
if you say oh
you keep everything in balance by yourself.

your lap and nightfall
rumbling of tinfoil
summit of us – where I sink
like the red and the black
that befits
a blood moon – that throws into confusion
the massive night – long gypsy
skirt – uprooted faith
but that raising of domes
relief of souls
may the wanting be a feather
mercy of the deep

uno scisma delicato
intrecciando le dita
come un filo di fiato.

non vere nozze
promette l'insieme - inventari
nomi comuni - antica europa
assediata nei coltivi a quadretti
del lungo suddividere
storia del catasto - orti di famiglia
noiosa tutela che fa poveri
anche voi
poemi didascalici: perché?
e perché loro - affranti
da un compito - per non scontrarsi
si amano
solo da lontano - luminosi pianeti?
una benedizione di luce
ci raggiunge - spolverio di strass
sulle tue guance
avvincente somigliare
da cui tanto chiamare in occidente.

a delicate schism
intertwining your fingers
like a wisp of breath.

not true nuptials
the whole promises – inventories
common names – old Europe
under siege in the checkered farmland
of the long subdivision
history of the land registry – family vegetable gardens
boring guardianship that makes poor
even all you
didactic poems: why?
and why them – grief stricken
by a task – in order to not collide
they love each other
only from afar – luminous planets?
a benediction of light
reaches us – a powdering of strass
on your cheeks
charming likeness
from which so much calls in the west.

3. il trapezista che volò

vanno materie volatili - la mente
città con tanti gatti
nel retro di cucine
lische di pesce - di nascosto dal mare
Gianni ti ho visto di tre quarti
camminavi con scarpe comode
(con passi più lunghi della fine)
ti domando: che differenza c'è
tra una donna e una madre?
pensa alla borsetta di vernice
la fodera di finta seta
Santina che dice: se almeno
avessi fatto la quinta!
a discolpa dell'origine
malfatti con le ortiche
e loro - ancora signorine?
con slanciate caviglie
già doppiato il discorso
voi - frasi degli immolati!
se ci pensi
non ci sono foto da bambini
(vuole dire che ci siamo inventati?)
vanagloria
quel fatto e finito
oh trasbordarvi - verso la fine del secolo
a piccoli gruppi - miei cari
(quelli che mangiavano insieme
sotto lumi a petrolio
nostra privata comunione)
un credo inestinguibile - come un'estinzione.

lo scampo non è
l'interezza - soltanto
ad occhi chiusi - beatitudini
come chi - furiosamente
si consegna
è questo

3. the trapeze artist who flew

unstable materials go – mind
city with so many cats
at the back of kitchens
fishbones – hidden from the sea
Gianni I saw you in three-quarters profile
you were walking with comfortable shoes
(with steps longer than the end)
I ask you: what difference is there
between a woman and a mother?
think of the patent leather purse
its lining of fake silk
Santina saying: if only I
had finished fifth grade!
in defense of the beginning
gnocchi made with nettles
and they – still young ladies?
with slender ankles
speech already dubbed
you – phrases of the immolated!
if you think about it
there are no photos of when we were kids
(does that mean we invented ourselves?)
vainglory
that over and done
oh transferring there – near the end of the century
in small groups – my loved ones
(those who ate together
under oil lamps
our private communion)
an undying faith – like an extinction

the way out is not
the entirety – just
with eyes closed – bliss
like someone who – furiously
surrenders
is this

l'ultimo significato
dell'utero?
Gianni ti ho visto con gli occhi
senza palpebre - sbiancati
nella luce impietosa
oh tu muovessi le ciglia come nuvole
sorprendente temporale
il bel rumore sull'ombrello
quando piove.

fa coppia - come rivolgersi
nell'intimo - come un dialogo
cuore del dire
dolencia de amor - que no se cura
(Juan) - è la voce
che conta - staccare le sillabe
pronunciare - o si perde il respiro
nel troppo largo - lasciato andare
come liberare uccellini
altre volte farfalle - sfarfallare
come il lento salire
di bollicine nell'acqua
l'oscuro solletico dei topolini
infinito spirare
(Gianni) è tardi
per guarire a casaccio
antidoti obsoleti - (la presencia y la figura)
invece
a tavolino ecco il nostro piano:
(in un batter d'occhio - si esalta
fino a niente la ramaglia appenninica
antico argento argille
lune agrarie - e voi
domiciliati in segreto - che di continuo
bisbigliate)
ecco che si alza la linea d'onda
caritatevole lontano - come un nulla
assenza senza offesa - occhio che la culla.

appena dopo - al seguito
tentarono di farla franca

the ultimate meaning
of the uterus?
Gianni I saw you with your eyes
without eyelids – turned white
in the pitiless light
oh if you would move your eyebrows like clouds
surprising thunderstorm
the beautiful sound on the umbrella
when it rains.

pair up – like turning
inward – like a dialogue
heart of the words
dolencia de amor – que no se cura
(Juan) – it's the voice
that counts – detaching the syllables
pronouncing – or you lose your breath
in the too wideness – let go
like freeing little birds
other times butterflies – wobbling
like the slow rise
of little bubbles in water
the mysterious tickle of the mice
infinite dying
(Gianni) it's late
for randomly recovering
obsolete antidotes – (*la presencia y la figura*)
instead
in theory here's our plan:
(in the blink of an eye – one praises
like nothing else the Apennines' brushwood
old silver clays
harvest moons – and you
living in secret – because of continuous
whispers)
this is why the line of the wave rises
benevolent distance – like a nothing
absence without offense – eye that cradles it.

right after – subsequently
they try to do it openly

ciuffolotti e ballerine
poi sorprese a non finire
da lontano la pinna di un pesce
tonni che salpano - tra piccole schiume
negli armadi
scarpette di vernice
qualcuno gridò:
il tempo sia neutrale
(spingono magliette - seni piccolini)
allora il tempo entrò - le femmine
stavano con le ginocchia unite - noi da soli
nei banchi dietro - diventati maschi.

tu li puoi conoscere - quando cedono
i segreti - con loro
ho parlato di continuo - in antico
abbiamo gettato la lancia
fianco a fianco - fratelli
ma tu amica mia - il tuo corpo
che tento di occupare - affinché rimangano
sconosciuti a te
e a me - vorrei dirti:
lascia che almeno lui
venga rischiarato - in quel riverbero
lascia un'impronta sul cuscino - con decoro
apri il tuo cuore - facci incontrare
in quell'ignoto - ausiliatrice.

anche il trapezista che volò
oltre il grappolo di lumi
finalmente fu invisibile
finalmente fu felice
ma colpito dal riflettore nel buio
con le braccia larghe come ali
apparve inventata figura
in quell'istante meritevole
idea e creatura
almeno ancora una volta
o almeno al telefono.

bullfinches and ballerinas
then no end of surprises
from afar a fish's fin
tunas that leap – among little foam bubbles
in the closets
patent leather heels
someone cried:
may time be neutral
(they press against sweaters – tiny breasts)
then time arrived – the girls
remained with their knees closed – we by ourselves
on the benches behind – having become men.

you could get to know them – when they yielded
their secrets – I spoke
with them continuously – in the old days
we cast the spear
side by side – brothers
but you my friend – your body
that I try to occupy – so that they would remain
unknown to you
and to me – I would like to tell you:
at least let him
become enlightened – in that glare
leave an imprint on the pillow – with decorum
open your heart – make us meet
in that unknown – oh helper.

and the trapeze artist who flew
beyond the cluster of lights
was finally invisible
was finally happy
but struck by the floodlight in the dark
with his arms broad like wings
he seemed an invented figure
in that worthy moment
idea and creature
at least once more
or at least on the phone.

troppo a lungo
chiamano con lo stesso nome
anche le madri
che partoriscono interamente
è una balla - quelle grida
per mantenere esseri interi
così piange - nascosta follia
vanno lacrime sul miele
spalmato sul pane
ma chi chiamò era vero
mi piacerebbe dirti
mi chiamo Matteo
partirò per un viaggio.

for too long
they call by the same name
even the mothers
who give birth completely
it's a lie – that screams
for keeping beings whole
and so it cries – hidden madness
tears fall into the honey
spread on the bread
but whoever called was right
I would have liked to tell you
my name is Matteo
I'll be leaving on a journey.

4. decennio

finalmente
niente sarà   altro abbastanza
magazzino di luci e polveri
c'è la pompa dello zolfo
un cartoccio di solfato di rame
nell'universo di palpebre in moto
tutto è al sicuro
tutto è immortale
c'è il pane   nel sacchetto sul tavolo
la farina   con accanto due uova
nel paesaggio   ci sono salici gentili
vecchi contadini
legano tralci   con dita musicali
bambini nella foresta di granoturco
come mai quel batticuore?
miti delitti
limpide piaghe   lasciò l'infanzia
bianche medicine
e frasi scure
essere materno   la mia nascita
ha interrotto te bambina?
bastassero mille torte di mele
per mettere in pari qualcosa
una parola sì e una no
in mezzo c'è il nostro restare
(oh granita con la neve
caduta a febbraio
sui pini dell'ospedale)
ecco:
il nostro pensiero ha un volume
come dire: un peso posato sul suolo
un luogo natale   una furia
quando vuole scappare
allora cos'è?
un monumento un cavallo di bronzo
che corre per sempre - nelle notti di neve?
pensa alle nevicate dei sensi - al continuo

4. decade

in the end
there will be nothing   different enough
storehouse of lights and powders
there's the pump for the sulfur
a bag of copper sulphate
in the universe of eyelids in motion
everything is in a safe place
everything is immortal
there's the bread   in its bag on the table
the flour   with two eggs beside it
in the landscape   there are gentle willows
old farmers
tie shoots   with musical fingers
children in the forest of corn
why is there that heartbeat?
myths crimes
clear sorrows   childhood left
white medicines
and somber phrases
maternal being   did my birth
interrupt you little girl?
it would take a thousand apple pies
to even up something
a yes and a no
in the middle there's our remaining
(oh granita made from snow
fallen in February
on the hospital's pines)
here:
our thought has a volume
that is to say: a weight set on the ground
a place of birth   a frenzy
when it wants to run away
well then what is it?
a monument a bronze horse
that runs forever – in the snowy nights?
think of the snowfalls of the senses – of the continuum

che bussa   al pettirosso d'inverno
ai portenti dell'amore
pensa al giocoliere e alla sua crisi
(con una palla di luce una palla di buio)
pensa a Maria
che va a trovare Elisabetta
pensa alle parentele   noi con poche zie poche cugine
poco da spiare negli specchi del comò
(padre ammutolito)
sul tavolo
un pacchetto di nazionali senza filtro
per dire che ero passato
e tu   capace di abitare i minuti
fiorisce davanti al rallentatore
la grande peonia
beatitudine in te   rugiada come perle
ecco   innescato l'inizio
collidono   esseri affrettati
abbracci bestiali   in macerie
finisce il decennio
mentre tutto s'ammucchia sui confini?
per questo sono in giubilo le vecchie lamiere?
l'io che abdicò non abbia successori
ciò che a torto fu scambiato
sia una riga illeggibile
oh la fine che allenta le mani
si scioglie il senso puro
che ci spinge molto più indietro
cade il verso in mucchietti di prosa
adesso è il momento di chiedere
se tutto va bene se serve qualcosa.

that knocks   of the winter robin
of the portents of love
think of the juggler and of his crisis
(with a ball of light and a ball of darkness)
think of Maria
who goes to visit Elisabetta
think of our relatives   we with few aunts few cousins
little to spy on in the dresser's mirrors
(father struck dumb)
on the table
a pack of unfiltered nationals
to say that I had passed through
and you   capable of dwelling in the minutes
flowering in slow motion
big peony
bliss within you   dew like pearls
here   the beginning triggered
they collide   beings in a hurry
beastly embraces   in ruins
does the decade end
while everything piles up at the edges?
is this why the old wrecks are rejoicing?
the *I* who abdicated may have no successors
that which was exchanged wrongly
may be an illegible line
oh the end that slows the hands
pure feeling dissolves
that pushes us much farther back
the verse falls into little piles of prose
now is the moment to ask
if everything's alright if something is needed.

5. oh voi dormienti angeli

nel tratto che intercorre non è il fine che fa ordine né vegliare o dormire è possibile né metterci una pezza quando l'uno è piegato in due è un interno con alti soffitti e tu non ridere o tutto il borotalco vola via manca una parete in quella casa sul pavimento c'è una scarpetta rovesciata se ti frughi in tasca troverai nocciolini di ciliegie vuole dire che è vero o che invece ti sei perso? oh generalmente o subito io o unito e lontano come è lontana la luna o l'argento così fossi punito rimmel dei tuoi occhi siano oscurati i primi piani tra le flottiglie di pesci che ti toccano soltanto la domanda rende veri? eccomi allora come il vero che sta in fila pensa agli anziani negli uffici postali pensa alle sale d'aspetto oh testa dell'angelo dormiente in questo limbo drogato girano corpi e figure indistinguibili oh lacerata retina come lacerarsi è guardare io ti chiamo ma dappertutto è chiamare come chi tornò dalle madri non sue le uniche possibili perdonate voi arcobaleni alte palme nella luce incrollabili nei ricoveri dell'intimo piccole ciotole e preghiere

come vivere a memoria è il deperire mirabile quando cala nell'imbrunire il sospiro del distinto nelle tue braccia consegno i prodotti del giorno oh spirata non più voce in quel trapasso vanno in pensiero le cose come va in semenza la cicoria madri di allora chi più di voi è diventato parola? negativi dei corpi sono le camicie vuote da stirare voi che staccate scagliette di gioia con l'unghia e sciogliete ostie nel cuore a cosa paragonare la vecchia borsa della spesa forse a un utero forse a un libro da studiare? bambini persi a moscacieca nel labirinto senza muri viaggi per mare e alti velieri cinema del pomeriggio e peccati mortali en aceite de olivas sardine portoghesi o me mucho o si fuera l'eterno che insiste nonostante l'addio il bel profilo di spalle la gru che attraversa l'europa se fosse ma anche se fosse la ultima vez meu amigo de alma.

l'aperto dove l'intimo saluta buon giorno e buona sera chi porta in giro la sua notte e le scure violette che allevò? io non è chiaro nel passaggio né il chiarore penetra un millimetro per cui spiovono luci sulle tue spalle figura che fai la parte di chimera dimmi pure angelo dell'etica guarda sempre in quel modo il grande male? nei cassetti c'è ancora l'odore di naftalina orco necessario che ci sei nessuno ti ha mai visto ma so che insegni il riserbo alla gioia e alle finte mete del mare quando trova la riva con schiaffi molli di onde che all'aperto cadevano

5. oh you sleeping angels

in the time in between it's not the end that puts things in order nor is waking or sleeping possible or patching something when one is bent over it's an interior with high ceilings and don't laugh or all the talcum powder will fly away one wall in that house is missing on the floor there's an overturned shoe if you rummage in your pocket you will find cherry pits does that mean it's true or rather that you're lost? oh generally either immediately I or close and as far as the moon is far or the silver so I would be punished oh your mascaraed eyes may be darkened up close between the flotillas of fish that just touch you does merely the question make us truthful? here I am then like the truth that's standing in line think of the old people in the post offices think of the waiting rooms oh head of the sleeping angel in this drugged limbo indistinguishable bodies and figures going around oh torn retina as if tearing is looking I call you but everywhere it's calling like someone who returned to mothers who were not theirs the only possible ones all you rainbows and tall palms in the indestructible light forgive me and my intimate shelters of the heart their little bowls and prayers.

like living by heart it's the admirable deterioration when at dusk the breath of the distinct falls into your arms I deliver the products of the day oh exhaled no longer voice in that passage do things become thought like chicory goes to seed mothers of that time who more than you has become word? negatives of the bodies are the empty shirts to iron you who break off little chips of joy with your fingernails and dissolve hosts in your heart what is there to compare with the old shopping bag maybe a uterus maybe a book to study? children lost to blind man's bluff in the maze without walls trips to the sea and tall sailing ships movies in the afternoon and mortal sins Portuguese sardines *en aceite de olivas* either *me mucho* or *si fuera* the eternal that insists despite the goodbye the beautiful outline of shoulders the crane that crosses Europe if it could but also if it were *la ultima vez meu amigo de alma.*

is the exterior where the inner self says good morning and good evening to someone who carries around his night and the dark violets he raised? *I* is not clear in the passageway nor does the glow penetrate a millimeter that's why lights fall down on your shoulders figure that plays the part of chimera just tell me angel of ethics does great evil always look like that? in the drawers there's

per farsi sollevare oh mie creste dell'onda! soltanto gli stronzi possono pensare: sono arrivate a casa finalmente! anche tu Albertina che lanci bacini con la mano per telefono quasi fossi un coetaneo invece sono come una poesia al poeta una differenza per sempre tu che hai appena fatto la terza mi sembra di averti già vista in un banco davanti alzavi le braccia per rifarti la coda di cavallo sembravi un'orante o una resa nuvole bianche di notte dicono che ci vuole distanza per vederle navigare e fuggire mentre continua a finire l'inizio.

evoluta più volte variabile anche la piccola sosta è un ritorno o una furia quando la mente è ancor più vedova mentre va via un fatto solitario? si odono disperati proclami verso sera: chi sopporta il tempo così a lungo senza essere contemporanei? oh ginocchio semiaperto sotto il manto di madonne un'avance è il ricordo di sempre mia mente bambina e i tuoi panneggi di parabole signora con più di cento rose un rossetto all'albicocca noi che fummo felici cuccioli con molte preghiere e molti battimani la domanda squillò come un applauso (sono volati via anche gli storni?) madri di compagni di scuola madonne con più seno davvero il tempo è un virus? mente febbrile che naviga nel sonno tra gli ostacoli rispondono passanti nel piacere quando l'oro si disfa nel suo viola ma al sicuro è rimasta la domanda senza cambiare una virgola si girano specchiere incorniciate di scuro vagano lunghe ciglia sull'acqua nella perdizione verso l'alba la mente che sta zitta.

mente collinosa guarda l'acqua incomprimibile: ha pensato ai pesci come propria liberazione da allora salgono bollicine divertenti (sarà ossigeno?) e loro che mai si fermano? non pensarci fidati! appartengono alla dimenticanza esseri ombra che guizzano ma noi no - per questo amiamo i tornanti le strade di langa e i crinali dell'oltrepò dall'alto delle curve si senta la nostra voce le sue plurime mansioni ivi compresi i fini ornamentali il chicchirichì dei maschi senza motivi plausibili inalberati vessilli ai brividini della luce che arranca dal collinoso orizzonte in brume e brine sarà un sacerdote colui che sbraita da pulpiti improvvisati con voce allibita lui stesso con i timpani rotti dal rimbombo che grida a più non posso adesso adesso!

still the smell of mothballs necessary ogre who's there no one ever saw you but I know that you teach reserve to joy and to the false destinations of the sea when it finds the shore with soft slapping of waves that fell on open waters to have themselves be raised oh my wave crests! only bastards can think: they finally arrived home! you too Albertina who throw little kisses with your hand by phone as if I were someone of the same age instead I am like a poem to the poet a difference forever you who have just finished the third year of high school I seem to have seen you before at a desk in front of me you were raising your arms to redo your ponytail you seemed to be praying or surrendering white clouds at night mean that there needs to be distance to see them to navigate and flee while the beginning continues to end.

the variable many times evolved is even the short stay a return or a fury when the mind is even more a widow while a single fact goes away? desperate proclamations toward evening are heard: who can stand such a long time without being contemporaries? oh half-open knee under the mantle of madonnas an advance is the same old memory oh my child mind and your drapery of parables oh lady with more than a hundred roses and apricot lipstick we who were happy puppies with many prayers and much handclapping the question rang like applause (did even the starlings fly away?) mothers of schoolmates madonnas with bigger breasts is time really a virus? feverish mind that navigates in sleep among the obstacles passers-by respond in pleasure when the gold melts into its violet but the question remained safe without changing a comma dark-framed mirrors spin long eyelashes wander over the water in the perdition before dawn the mind that remains quiet.

hilly mind look at the incompressible water: did it think of the fish as its own liberation since then amusing little bubbles have risen (might it be oxygen?) and they that never stop? don't think about it trust! they belong to forgetting shadowy beings that dart but we no – this is why we love the hairpin turns the hilly streets and the ridges beyond the Po from the height of the curves our voice can be heard its multiple mansions there including the ornamental goals the males' cock-a-doodle-doo without plausible reasons banners raised up in the little shudders of the light that struggles along from the hilly horizon in mist and frost he might be a priest he who brays from improvised pulpits with astounded voice with his own eardrums broken by the booming that cries at the top of his voice now now!

sommariamente contati invece sono cubici tutti gli esseri che gridano eccoci senza le pareti (lo vuole la legge?) adesso siamo scatoloni appiattiti - ma quando arriva l'autunno dove conservano i bambini le figure i vasetti dei ricordi come in vasetti è il sole sotto vetro? io dico: di questi chicchi in fila uno è il semprevivo dei tetti l'altro è il giorno che disse questo è il giorno che fu mentre sono già assenti le donne che sgranavano fave o piselli alt! voi che seminate discredito sulla debolezza della fine su ciò che è troppo simile quasi uguale il doppio e il triplo! gemono sotto il linguaggio che li svergogna miei poemi! mai arrivati alla colpa immolati invano nel sovversivo frufru dell'inaudito ora non si sente rumore di piatti dalla finestra aperta valido è soltanto il titolo mentre cade l'ombra ai tuoi piccoli piedi vecchie maestre piangono i caduti.

they are cursorily numbered rather they are cubic all the beings who cry here we are without walls (does the law require it?) now we are big flattened boxes – but when autumn arrives do they keep the children the figures the jars of memories just as the sun is in jars under glass? I say: of these beans in a row one is the everlasting of the rooftops the other is the day that said this is the day that was while already missing are the women who shelled beans or peas stop! you who sow discredit on the weakness of the end on that which is too similar almost equal its double and its triple! they moan under the language that shames them my poems! never reaching offense sacrificed in vain in the subversive frou-frou of the unheard-of now no noise of plates is heard from the open window only the title is valid while the shadow falls at your little feet old teachers mourn the fallen.

trattatello incostante / variable treatise
(1980)

1. raccontino da fermo

almeno lasciami sembrare, città,
come le tue strade vuote di domenica
le vie del cielo che ridicono: tutto l'esistente
è benzina sul fuoco!
lasciami partecipare, ti chiedo,
con tutte le mie parentesi chiuse,
(ehi sono io - infine ti dirò)
(sono l'aria sotto la tua gonna)
parole con le quali
da tanto mi percuoto
come la finestra che sbatte
mentre non tira un filo d'aria.

se tu vedessi, milanesa,
lo stile delle tue ginocchia
chi vuoi che pensi
al tuo astuccio dei colori
all'elastichino nei capelli
se non chi per niente
toccava i setti cieli?
non saprei cosa dire
in merito al pieno e al vuoto
fino al cavalcavia di via Meda
questo attardarsi
nello spazio comune
dove nessuno chiede niente
benevolenza dell'ignoto
all'improvviso è un fuggi fuggi
chi prende le calze i fazzoletti
già da questo puoi capire.

sono uscito per vederti
in questo stato critico
come se la gioia
fosse la prova del nove?
con le aste e i puntini
suprema chiarezza
chicchi di miglio

1. little story standing still

at least let it seem to me, city
like your empty Sunday streets
the pathways of the sky that repeat: everything that exists
is fuel on the flames!
let me participate, I ask,
with all my parentheses
(hey it's me – I'll finally tell you)
(I am the air under your skirt)
words with which
I've beaten myself for so long
like the window that slams
while not even a wisp of air blows.

if you were to see, girl of Milan,
the style of your knees
who would you want to think
of your case of colors
of the elastic band in your hair
but those who had for the least of things
touched the seven heavens?
I wouldn't know what to say
about the fullness and the emptiness
until the overpass on Via Meda
this lingering
in the common space
where no one asks anything
benevolence of the unknown
suddenly it's go go
someone takes stockings handkerchiefs
from this alone you can understand.

did I go out to see you
in this critical state
as if joy
were the acid test?
with the strokes and dots
supreme clarity
grains of millet

luminosi granellini
perché dunque? il viso schiacciato
contro la gonna della maestra?

è adesso che vorrei trasformare
i sospiri in quel viavai
di orecchini
i tuoi sonagli senza audio
come le ciglia che si alzano
e i laghetti di luce
pupille
se io fossi una conseguenza
grazie tante lo stesso
(può durare più di un'ora)
la chiesa di San Gottardo
è un'alcova, Anna
dove si dissanguano
preghiere
immuni dal linguaggio
che distingue
irresistibile bisbiglio
perdona se non so usare
lo shock che portiamo nel cuore
i socialisti hanno fallito
per primi?
e il tuo sguardo?
non guardarmi - avevo implorato
se ci pensi è la resa perfetta
la nostra posizione di lato.

sei tu la tapparella che si alza
in questa mattina espansiva
la caffettiera che borbotta
di domenica
sono qui con il corpo
al posto del pensiero
a questo punto
non c'è un minuto da perdere
chiunque può fare una strage.

si complica la cosa da sola
(sembra incredibile)

luminous granules
why then? the face flattened
against the teacher's skirt?

it's now that I'd like to transform
the sighs in that coming and going
of earrings
your rattling without audio
like the eyebrows that rise
and the little lakes of light
your pupils
if I were a consequence
thanks so much all the same
(it can last more than an hour)
the church of San Gottardo
is an alcove, Anna
where prayers
bleed to death
immune from the language
that characterizes
irresistible whispering
pardon me if I don't know how to use
the shock that we carry in our hearts
did the socialists fail
first?
and your gaze?
don't look at me — I would beg
if you think about it it's the perfect surrender
our position aside.

you are the blinds that rise
on this expansive morning
the coffee pot that rumbles
on Sunday
I am here with my body
in place of thought
at this point
there's not a minute to lose
anyone could cause a disaster.

the thing gets complicated on its own
(it seems incredible)

se nessuno la mette in riga
fatta e finita
cosa odierna - che deve bastare
sia breve l'intervallo
tra le sillabe - infinito in agguato
senti che sbuca dalla nebbia
un gigantesco cavallo
il suo zoccolo d'osso
un secco tamburo?

non te lo dico interamente
(è a tuo vantaggio - se ci pensi)
(a nascondino mi trovi in un minuto)
o subito alla fine fischia
infantile sillabare
indicare con il dito
notizie indistinguibili
(ogni espressione
cambia i connotati)
(nella fototessera
il viso è già stravolto)
(oh pazienti poemi)
in quest'ultima rivolta del bene
i più miti da soli si pungono il cuore
oh almeno! - siano ben spesi
gli assoluti più piccoli
biglie di vetro colorato
in giusta dose - il rosso puro.

ma tu produci frasi davvero
(ti ho sentita)
(imburrare hai detto
poi lasci riposare)
parole con cose - fanno una catena
(oh il patto di mancare!
la fedeltà degli orfanelli!)
(mentre imperversa il positivo)
maglioncini girocollo
precipizi tra persone
(tu sei potente potente)
nebbiosa città
inguine silenziosa

if no one puts it right
over and done
today's thing – that must be enough
may the gap be short
between the syllables – infinitive lying in wait
do you hear emerging from the fog
a gigantic horse
its hoof of bone
a sharp drum?

I won't tell you completely
(it's to your advantage – if you think about it)
(you'll find me evasive in a minute)
or right at the end let it go
childish spelling
pointing with my finger
indistinguishable news
(every expression
changes the features)
(in the ID photo
the face is already contorted)
(oh patient poems)
in this last revolt of goodness
the meekest prick the heart on their own
oh at least! – may they be well spent
the smallest absolutes
colored glass marbles
in the right amount – the red pure.

but you produce real sentences
(I've heard you)
(buttering you said
then you let it rest)
words with things – make a chain
(oh the pact of missing!
the faithfulness of the little orphans!)
(while the positive rages)
crew-neck sweaters
abysses between people
(you are powerful powerful)
foggy city
silent groin

unghie lucenti contro il buio
cinque anelli nelle dita.

prima o poi arriva - l'improvviso
mentre mettono
pezza su pezza i viventi
che si guardano - qualcuno dice
vieni!
c'è una foto dell'amata
nel portafoglio dei camionisti
le ragazze si parlano all'orecchio
stringente sillogismo
il pube - orlo delle mutandine
chiamata degli eletti
eppure erano insieme
nel banco di terza
lei ancora con le cosce magre
mastica la matita - aspetta l'interrogazione
poi gli tolse
una pagliuzza dalla manica
e suonarono tutte insieme
le campane dell'incoronazione.

ti direi che colma
di grazia - interamente nata
sei tu - quella che attraversò
tutti i nomi comuni
sovrabbondanza che si dispera
improvvisa come uno slancio
la gonna sopra il ginocchio
fu come un grido provocante
la riga bassa a sinistra
gli occhi disegnati a matita
traballante trampoliere
la prima volta sui tacchi.

sottile stagnola lamiere
piccolissimi tuoni
preliminari di qualche piacere
ci protegga la densità
(i contrapposti

fingernails shining in the dark
five rings on your fingers.

sooner or later it arrives – suddenly
while they are putting
piece onto piece the living
who are looking – someone says
come!
there's a photo of the loved one
in the truck drivers' wallets
the girls talk into their ears
urgent syllogism
the pubis – edge of the panties
the call of the chosen
and yet they were together
at the third-year desk
she with her thighs still skinny
chewing her pencil – waiting for the questioning
then she took
a speck from her sleeve
and the coronation bells
sounded all together.

I would tell you that it fills
with gracefulness – fully born
you are – she who passes through
all the common names
excess that loses hope
suddenly like a rush
the skirt above the knee
was like a provocative cry
the low stripe on the left
the eyes drawn with pencil
wobbling wading bird
the first time in heels.

thin sheet of foil
very small thundering
preliminaries to some pleasure
may the thickness protect us
(the opposites

che fanno combriccola)
cause e sorprese
un mix accettabile
non lasciare troppo tempo
tra una cosa e l'altra
quella bocca spalancata
era un drago.

ma a te direi (più che a chiunque):
fidati!
il tuo filo che mi tiene
lo seguo a ritroso
(fino alla madonna della neve
a papa giovanni sul comò)
(solo tu conosci
l'evento più antico)
madre timorosa
dimmi la verità: mi hai sognato
che tornavo - ma non ero partito
per questo mantengo
il segreto
l'inizio perduto che esclama
non sono nemmeno iniziato!

ciò non toglie che tu
continui a colmare
quel buco primigenio
con le cose più strane
(somiglianti - ma dispari)
attesi retroscena - torta paradiso
la polvere di zucchero a velo
la bustina di lievito Bertolini
mentre lasci in giro
l'uvetta - nel caso
si svegliassero i bambini.

si muovono per compenso
anche i cieli - depressione
che chiama fiumi d'aria
ehi
piccoli soffi marginali

that make up a clique)
causes and surprises
an acceptable mix
don't leave too much time
between one thing and another
that gaping mouth
was a dragon.

but to you I would say (more than to anyone):
have confidence!
your thread that holds me
I follow backwards
(to the madonna of the snow
to pope john on the dresser)
(only you know
the oldest event)
timid mother
tell me the truth: you dreamed
that I had returned – but I had not left
this is why I keep
the secret
the lost beginning that exclaims
I haven't even begun!

the fact remains that you
continue to fill up
that primordial hole
with the strangest things
(similar – but unequal)
expectations behind-the-scenes – cake paradise
the dusting of sprinkled sugar
the envelope of Bertolini yeast
while you leave the raisins
around – in case
the children wake up.

even the heavens move
in compensation – depression
that calls rivers of air
well
little secondary puffs

riccioli dopo lo shampoo
soffice palla
è il vento di pasqua
(lei apre la finestra finzione)
vicina a un corpo
è qualunque parola
magari una sorpresa
lei stessa in persona.

cosa chiedeva?
primo: piuttosto basterebbe
iniziare - quinto piano
cinque rampe di scale
corpo - che è sempre totale
tu sì ma chiesa - principio
di astrazione - oro fulvo
buio in comunione
vicino al vero - nostra imitazione
colonne tortili
con più di mille ragioni.

come funzioni - o involucri
scatole di latta dipinta
(biscotti inglesi per te)
(poi ci metterai gomitoli di lana)
eccoci - dolorosi
fare gesti felici
assenti - per essere interi
con perfetta memoria - smemorati.

in sintesi:
oh buche umane - inalberata primavera
ben presto richiamato - brevissimo altro
belle facce umane leggendarie
e tu
per piccoli tumulti - lucentina
gioia immatura - nel vuoto cielo
disperata - infine
non a te
compete l'insieme
(suo magnifico errore)
bellavista.

curls after shampooing
a soft ball
it's the wind of easter
(she opens the window pretense)
near a body
is any sort of word
maybe a surprise
she herself in person

what was she asking?
first: or it would be enough
to begin – fifth floor
five flights of stairs
body – which is always entirely
you – but church – beginning
of abstraction – tawny gold
darkness in communion
close to the truth – our imitation
twisted columns
with more than a thousand reasons.

like functions – or packaging
painted tin boxes
(English biscuits for you)
(then you'll put balls of wool there)
here we are – sorrowful
making happy gestures
absent – for being complete
with perfect memory – forgetful.

in short:
oh human holes – springtime having risen
very soon recalled – something else very short
beautiful faces human legendary
and you
through little commotions – sparkling
immature joy – in the empty sky
despairing – in the end
it's not up
to you, the whole
(its magnificent error)
oh panorama!

2. imitazioni e preghiere

I
osservante
(tre volte approfondito)
così niente sarà
estremamente (o colpito)
sottosopra s'ingegna
più soave il minimo
il candido pensato
come fosse
in calmi dolori uguagliato.

2. imitations and prayers

I
observant
(up close three times)
so that nothing would be
extremely (or struck)
upside down one strives
the minimum softer
the candid thought
as if it were
equalized by calm pains.

II
così che quando fiammeggia
più esposto
ultimo cielo
(se dire
è come avvenire
nelle tue braccia perire)
ancora una volta
la calza è rovesciata
nella bella trama
amante ricaduto
mentre torna
l'inizio mai finito.

II
so that when it's aflame
more exposed
last heaven
(if saying
is like happening
in your arms perishing)
once again
the stocking inside out
in the beautiful plot
lover fallen
while there returns
the unfinished beginning.

III
conforme
clemente distrazione
lettere ti scriverei da lontano
(ma sul posto) (festa
che dimentica parole)
dire è disdire
grimaldello dell'inizio
celeste sorpasso
anteriori tuberi acque
o lingua che risale
da sola, fontana
come scema
più buia si consola.

III
in conformity
merciful distraction
letters I would write you from afar
(but on the spot) (holiday
that forgets words)
saying is retracting
picklock of the beginning
heavenly overtaking
earlier tubers waters
language that's rising
on its own, fountain
like a fool
consoling itself more darkly.

IV
predetto non sarà (ma contraddetto)
quel lungo custodire
piuttosto divenire (direi)
(ombra di un flash)
anima forse
il somigliante
(pregio dell'indugio)
non vana dimora
mia signora
con tanto sfarzo accaduto.

IV
it will not be predicted (but contradicted)
that long guarding
rather becoming (I would say)
(shadow of a flash)
soul perhaps
similar thing
(value of the delay)
not a modest dwelling
my lady
with so much evident dazzle.

V
movimentato
misericordioso volando
è di lusso
lacrime di remissione saranno
altarini dei caduti
non disadorne cicatrici
somigliante vulva
arcana guarigione
sotto le ciglia di un fatto
a mala pena accaduti.

V
animated
merciful flying
it's a luxury
there will be tears of forgiveness
little altars of the fallen
scars not bare
vulva likeness
mysterious recovery
under the eyebrows of an event
we only just happened.

VI
non indolore sarà
(passare dalla tua parte)
le storie
sono tutte evasioni?
allora perché brilla
sulla tovaglia
il bicchiere di cristallo
perché cade l'anima
in tante cascatelle
quando suoni alla porta?

VI
it will not be painless
(moving to your side)
the stories
are all of them escapes?
then why does it shine
on the tablecloth
the crystal drinking glass
why does the soul fall
in so many little waterfalls
when you ring at the door?

VII
sempre si dirige
né ha fine l'arrivo
veloce biancore
in questi salici
è il vento
mentre guardi
quelle fughe fittizie
come l'alba nell'imbrunire
fogliame che galoppa
senza mai fuggire.

VII
it always sets out
nor's arrival its purpose
swift whiteness
in these willows
it's the wind
as you look at
those fictitious flights
like dawn at sunset
foliage that runs wild
without ever escaping.

VIII
è probabile:
ti fa simile a sé
il conosciuto
l'intimo
svelato da ferite
oh santa teresa del bambino gesù
una scaglia di cosa
una ressa amorosa
incredibile tu!

VIII
it's probable:
it makes you similar to itself
the known
the inner
revealed by wounds
oh saint theresa of the baby jesus
a sliver of something
a loving throng
incredible you!

IX
un altro nascondiglio
è descrivere
fatto che taglia in mezzo
tromba che atterrisce
racconti in casa delle vedove
troppo poco è il presente
pensieri per conto loro
oscuri passeri
oscuri chicchi beccando.

IX
another hiding place
is describing
an act that cuts in two
a trumpet that terrifies
tales in the widows' house
the present is too little
thoughts on their own
dark sparrows
pecking at dark grains.

X
l'educazione che trattiene
per non perdere il filo
il tremendo quasi uguale
chi responsabile e invano
con le braccia alzate
gridò: non andrà che lontano!
allora direi a un mio bambino
preserva il vuoto con le azioni
così che il mondo
volando nel vuoto
volando da te
tu prendilo al volo
con in tasca un sacchetto
di lacrime d'oro.

X
the manners that hold back
so as not to lose the thread
the awful almost equal
someone responsible and in vain
with their arms raised
cried: he will only go far!
then I would say to my child
preserve the void with actions
so that the world
flying in the void
flying to you
you catch it in midair
with a pouch in your pocket
of golden tears.

3. trattatello incostante

tu non tornare
(lingua che ritorna)
proprio tu - singola
per sempre - freccia già partita
tu non ribadire
(è ciò che vogliono)
ma gli introvati - cercali
i tuoi fedeli che balbettano
non sono mai doppie le cose
i gerani dei quali si sente parlare
i pergolati di rose.

non è vero
che siamo iniziati
è il prima che continua
corre da uno all'altro
l'apparire - a grandi balzi
l'amore
questo rumore è l'acqua
che incanta il suo andare
sempre domenicale
è la descrizione
(non uscire dai bordi
quando colori i papaveri)
lei teneva il libro aperto
sulle ginocchia aguzze
ha consegnato il foglio di bella
mentre va via saltella.

se avessi gli occhi della mosca
le sue zampette sulla goccia di sudore
dove comincia l'io
tra fittizi confini?
non so se l'odore
della tua pelle mi porta
verso di te fino al cuore
o se ti respiro da lontano

3. variable treatise

you, don't return
(language that returns)
precisely you – separate
forever – arrow having already left
you, do not confirm
(that's what they want)
but the unfound ones – look for them
your followers who stutter
things are never doubled
the geraniums you hear spoken of
the pergolas of roses.

it's not true
that we have begun
it's the first one that continues
it runs from one to the other
the appearing – with big leaps
love
the sound is the water
that enchants its passing
always on Sunday
it's the description
(don't go outside the lines
when you color the poppies)
she would hold the book open
on her pointy knees
she handed over the best sheet
as she went off skipping.

if I had the eyes of a fly
its little legs on a drop of sweat
where does the *I* begin
within fictitious borders?
I don't know if the scent
of your skin carries me
toward you to your heart
or if you breathe from afar

come il grande pretesto
vicino alle tue ciglia
scure tendine del mistero
dove anch'io chiudo gli occhi
moscacieca.

dove finisce il nascosto
non è più lui che appare
usurpatore - è il visibile
che non perdona
per questo corro ai tuoi piedi
madonna della guardia
tu che riporti tutto
allo stato originale
dammi un segnale
in quella casa così sola
almeno il rumore del secchio
verso sera
quando è ora di innaffiare.

diversificare il soggetto
in corso d'opera - fare
un finto finale
stare alla larga
dall'ultimo
non competere
con chi può durare
sia incipiente qualcosa
anche più volte in un minuto
ecco i consigli pratici
per passare i doganieri
mai addurre
l'esistente come prova
(la presenza intera
è pari alla mancanza)
ma si può dire a chi c'è
non a chi manca.

in gioco - anche la nascita
(salta passaggi la rivoluzione?)
una vestina un bavagliolo

like the great opportunity
near your eyebrows
dark curtains of mystery
where I also close my eyes
blind man's buff.

where the hidden ends
it's no longer he who seems
the usurper – it's the visible
that does not forgive
this is why I run to your feet
madonna della guardia
you who restore everything
to its original state
give me a sign
in that house so alone
at least the sound of the pail
toward evening
when it's time to water.

differentiating the subject
during the execution – making
a fake ending
staying away
from the final one
does not compete
with someone who can last
it may be something incipient
even many times in a minute
here's the practical advice
for passing through customs
never produce
what exists as proof
(the whole presence
is equal to the absence)
but it can be said to someone who is there
not to someone who is missing.

at stake – even birth
(does the revolution skip passages?)
a baby's garment a bib

trombette per bambini
e la ninna nanna?
amate madri - inganni del neonato
(adesso segue con gli occhi
un cardellino)
(medita la fuga?) - mente oceano
barchette di un guscio di noce
bel bambino?

di questo dovremmo parlare
(non del pensiero narrativo)
(era un piazzale dei camion?)
gigantesca fu la pausa
(scaccia l'asfalto di agosto
l'ombra del privato)
arido sesso del cielo
(il senso si mostra
se c'è una sparizione?)
colpito
da incomprese frecce
Sebastiano
si commuove
una santa carnale
da finestre si vedono cucine
un fornello a due bocche
la caffettiera napoletana
tra ciò che rassomiglia - chi
ti trova?
oh buon Gesù
non darmi tempo - chiudimi tu!

sarà vero
come un vero di recupero
verso il senso
come ci si stanca!
volano via
i tendoni della proloco
(si è messo a piovere?)
(non arriva più nessuno?)
(i desideri più piccoli
sono diventati furiosi?)

trumpets for children
and the nursery rhyme?
beloved mothers – tricks of the newborn
(now it's following a goldfinch
 with its eyes)
(is it considering escape?) – mind ocean
a little cockleshell boat
beautiful child?

we should talk about this
(not about the narrative thought)
(was it a truckyard?)
the pause was gigantic
(the asphalt of August drives away
 the private person's shadow)
arid sex of the sky
(does meaning show itself
if there's a disappearance?)
struck
by misunderstood arrows
Sabastiano
touched was
a carnal *santa*
from the windows you could see kitchens
a stove with two burners
the Neapolitan coffee pot
among what it resembles – who
finds you?
sweet Jesus oh
don't give me time – finish me now!

it may be true
like a recovered truth
toward the meaning
how one tires of it!
they fly away
the tents of the village fair
(did it start to rain?)
(is no one else coming?)
(have the smallest desires
become wild?)

fogli di giornale
(per avvolgere le aringhe)
al volo - parole
strappate
appese ai ganci - violate
oh allegre sfigurate
(salvate - dall'orco peggiore
di ognuno)
mentre tutti gli sfrattati
organizzano un raduno.

perché?
volto dell'anima
ti rivolgi a quel profilo
ai suoi zigomi alti
illuminati da un fiammifero?
mia destinazione - chiesa
carnale - ombre scure
con orli d'oro
non osceni
i tuoi altari
ma il troppo vero
esplode - credimi
(guarda la baraonda i fruttivendoli)
acropolis - città di mare
corpo sconsacrato
un quarto d'ora d'orologio
il tempo di salmodiare.

sheets of newspaper
(to wrap up the herrings)
in flight – words
torn
hung on hooks – violated
oh happy disfigured
(saved – from everyone's
 worst ogre)
while all the evictees
organize a meeting.

why?
face of the soul
are you turning toward that profile
toward its high cheekbones
illuminated by a match?
my destination – carnal
church – dark shadows
with edges of gold
not obscene
your altars
but the too-true
explodes – believe me
(look at the bustle of the fruit vendors)
acropolis – city of the sea
deconsecrated body
a quarter hour on the clock
the time to sing psalms.

4. candid camera

quando siamo rimasti in due
siamo diventati insufficienti
abbiamo giocato a biglie
ma erano lacrime di vetro
la bravura è mancare il bersaglio
come assicura il lanciatore di coltelli
a volte basta una tovaglia
come se fosse di domenica
quando tirò il sasso nello specchio
non avrebbe immaginato di sparire.

appare qualcosa - e non significa l'amata
con cento rimedi vaneggia - favoloso sapere
(vuoi fare il contenuto? fai il palo?)
(o l'amore guardiano
mentre fa il suo giro?)
soltanto l'accaduto è abitato
grandissime dalie
(segni delle donne)
(aiuole di civiltà mature)
manca un colpo da maestro?
un riquadro di finestra – da dove riguardare?

mentre si prepara qualcosa
da qualche parte - a quest'ora
ci sono i minuti contati
sale d'aspetto - che di notte
chiudono alle due
e se dopo ci fosse il mare?
se non fosse Cesano Boscone
ma spalancato vuoto
tra acqua e cielo?
alla finestra - un rumore di vele
poi cieli mutevoli - soffitti dipinti
belli come i seni del respiro
dunque è vero: sei tu che non finivi
le equazioni per paura dell'uguale?

4. candid camera

when there were two of us left
we became insufficient
we played marbles
but they were tears of glass
the skill is missing the target
as the knife thrower guarantees
sometimes a tablecloth is enough
as if it were Sunday
when he threw the stone into the mirror
he wouldn't have imagined it disappearing.

something appears – and it does not mean the loved one
raving with a hundred remedies – fabulous knowledge
(do you want to do the contents? are you acting as lookout?)
(or guardian love
while it makes its rounds?)
only the event is inhabited
very big dahlias
(signs of the women)
(flowerbeds of mature civilizations)
is a masterly stroke missing?
a windowpane – from which to have another look?

while something is being prepared
somewhere – at this hour
there are the counted minutes
waiting rooms – that at night
close at two
and if after there were the sea?
if there were no Cesano Boscone
but a wide open void
between water and sky?
at the window – the sound of sails
then changeable sky – painted ceilings
beautiful like the breasts of breathing
and so is it true: is it you who did not finish
the equations for fear of the equal sign?

proteggevi le persone tra parentesi
antiche donne - con grandi grembiuli
mio amato
non voglio arrivare - in fondo al problema
non voglio quell'altro sapere
senso compiuto che fa presto a finire.

rimargina
il risultato - visto nell'insieme
foresta con tutte le foglie
poi uomini e donne
tantissimi - meno delle foglie
ma tanti - luci azzurrine
ciabatte bianche a buchini
turni di notte delle infermiere
potente infanzia - pensiero ardito
a scuola
chiamati per nome - gli abbandonati
godono il loro nome inaudito
adesso la collisione è vicina
scattano viticci - serpenti
nelle nobili vigne - tutti i quadri
sono fuori dalle cornici
break per carità
break - specie senza cuore
che osa continuare!

you were protecting the people in parentheses
ancient women – with big aprons
my beloved
I don't want to get – to the bottom of the problem
I don't want that other knowledge
completed meaning that's hurrying to end.

it heals
the result – seen as a whole
forest with all the leaves
then men and women
so many – fewer than the leaves
but many – pale blue lights
white slippers with holes
the nurses' night shifts
powerful childhood – daring thought
at school
called by name – the abandoned
enjoy their unheard-of name
now the collision is near
tendrils dart – snakes
in the noble vines – all the paintings
are outside the frames
break for heaven's sake
break – species without a heart
that dares to continue!

cosa bella cosa / thing beautiful thing
(1977)

1
a un millimetro dal corpo
(chi ti trova?) - tra un milione
indovina cucù

il senso che seguiva le persone
ha già passato via Custodi

affiora il profondo
in divertenti bollicine
apericena
con tante tartine

spergiuro esclamativo
che spegne ogni cerino

(troppo presto
 fatto ruffiano)

(va e viene dagli occhi
 luce che non guarda)

(oh bel volto
 che illumini Milano)

coperchi smaltati
di vecchie lampadine
nelle notti di vento
fantasmi sui muri.

1
at a millimeter from the body
(who finds you?) – out of a million
he guesses cuckoo

the feeling that it was following people
already passed Via Custodi

the bottom comes to the surface
in amusing little bubbles
aperitif
with so many canapés

exclamatory perjury
that extinguishes every taper

(too soon
 bootlicking fact)

(it comes and goes from the eyes
 light that does not look)

(oh beautiful face
 that enlightens Milan)

enameled tops
of old lightbulbs
on the windy nights
ghosts on the walls.

2
all'uscita del cinema
zoccoli e ferri - sono ancora i cavalli?
sui selciati di Porta Vigentina
lentamente muoiono figure
(sempre un po' di più
dura un'idea)
(ma adesso è quasi sera)
ti lascio
il caffè sul tavolo
(oh asse verniciata
del grande naufragio)
(si vede ancora
la scritta Isabella)
infine arriva
il momento dei bari
(due finte e una vera
grida il giocoliere nella fiera)
è allora che bisogna
girare il tavolo
giocare con le carte della spia
o mentre stavi nella verità
come una culla
la domanda cambiava
e lei diventava una bugia.

2
upon leaving the movies
hooves and horseshoes – are there still horses?
on the pavements of Porta Vigentina
figures slowly die
(an idea always lasts
a little longer)
(but now it's almost evening)
I'll leave
the coffee on the table for you
(oh varnished planks
of the great shipwreck)
(you can still see
the writing Isabella)
finally the moment
arrives for the card sharps
(two fake and one real
shouts the juggler at the fair)
it's then that you need
to turn the table
play with the cards of the spy
or while you were in truth
like a cradle
the question changed
and she became a lie.

3
passerotto mio caro piumoso
così bello il tuo nome piumotto
esultare una volta non basta
o l'amore che toglie l'errore
certo che esiste stai calmo

il tatto non tocca
l'idea non sblocca
la verità è scadente
la canzone demente
questo e quest'altro ti piace?
le notizie i soldi fatti sotto
(così volendo nascere
op! op!
faceva le smorfie con la lingua
mangiava il fuoco le lamette)

(s'allontana l'ultima corriera
sembrano ballare i rossi fanalini
il verbo essere saluta con la mano
da dietro i finestrini).

3
my dear feathery little sparrow
so beautiful your quilted name
rejoicing once is not enough
or the love that error removes
certain that it exists stay calm

feeling does not touch
the idea's not released
the truth is second rate
the song demented
do you like this and that?
ouch news and money - come on
(so wanting to be born
hey! hey!
making faces with his tongue
he'd eat fire and razor blades.)

(the last bus went off
the red taillights seemed to dance
the verb *to be* waves with its hand
from behind the windows.)

4
>   (apri l'uscio apri l'uscio
>   c'è il presente senza guscio)

adesso sono visibili foglie di zucca
filari di fagioli
(è prevista
una descrizione per il lungo?)
(per tutto il tempo? per stare alla pari?)
(senza mai finire?)
ma dove parole e cose si biforcano
arde fuori di sé
la mente nel suo cielo
precipita la piccola fine
sembrano strilli di gioia
vano è il grande restare
tenere il posto occupato
mentre batte le palpebre l'amato
svanisce
l'oscuro che ci ha salvato.

4
                              (open the door open the door
                              it's the present without a shell)

the pumpkin leaves are visible now
all the rows of beans
(did you expect
a lengthy description?)
(for the whole time? for staying on par?)
(without ever ending?)
but where words and things bifurcate
there burns beside itself
the mind in its heaven
the little end hastens
they seem like shrieks of joy
vain is the great remaining
keeping the space occupied
while the lover beats his eyelids
it vanishes
the darkness that saved us.

5
potrebbe essere quella la scena:
lei che lava i piatti
il grembiule sulle anche magre
(attendere
è diventare colpevoli)
(chi non è subito
diventa un altro)
così non so
se quello era il tuo seno
sotto quel grembiule
se c'ero anch'io.

5
that could be the scene:
she washing the dishes
the apron on her narrow hips
(to wait
is to become guilty)
(someone who didn't immediately
become another)
so I don't know
if that was your bosom
under that apron
if I was there too.

6
c'era da aspettarselo:
il tempo si mangia i tavoli le sedie
inutile fermarlo con le mani
ma sul suo corpo si calmava
le unghie brillavano nei sandali
le gambe si innalzavano.

6
it was to be expected:
time devours the table the chairs
it's useless to stop it with your hands
but regarding her body it grew calm
her nails shone in the sandals
her legs rose.

7
incomprensibile borotalco fine fine
nuvola di paradiso
camera dei genitori
cassetti dei misteri
sul chi vive
bambini
parole padrone
lacrime strane
sulla cipria rosa
profumi Paglieri.

7
incomprehensible very fine talcum powder
cloud of paradise
the parents' room
drawers of mysteries
on the alert
children
under master words
strange tears
over the pink powder
Paglieri perfumes.

8
siliqua sistro sonaglio
banda di gusci di ceci
a quintali vocali fagioli
nelle stoppie la quaglia
le mele nella paglia
giocando si può dire
la ginestra che è gialla
l'azzurra farfalla
cosa bella cosa
nome senza cosa
cosa che non osa
mondo bel mondo
buio senza fondo
è micidiale lì fuori
senza una parola
e tu devi esclamare esclamare.

8
sistrum rattle silicles
band of chickpea shells
vocal beans by the ton
in the brush the quail
the apples in the hay
playing you could say
the Spanish broom that's yellow
the blue butterfly
thing beautiful thing
name without thing
thing that doesn't dare
world beautiful world
darkness without end
it's lethal there outside
without a word
and you must cry out cry out.

9
se senti il colpo del tram
sugli scambi - è un buon segno
(come uno scopo) verso sera
dice che il giorno sospira
che la notte si mette
i suoi begli orecchini
con distrazioni si affronta
il mondo in generale
(pan per focaccia
per così dire)
oh mia piccola quaglia!
con la trombetta nel grano
esattamente vuole apparire
sotto l'azzurro vuole perire
ha l'anima infervorata
ha la testa sbagliata
vuole l'aperta verità
la proclama e non l'avrà
(ne avrà solo la metà)
come giusta punizione
lo sparviero la mangerà.

9
if you hear the bump of the tram
on the switch – it's a good sign
(like a goal) toward evening
she says that the day breathes
that the night puts on
its beautiful earrings
with distractions one
faces the world in general
(tit for tat
so to speak)
oh my little quail!
with its trumpet in the wheat
it wants to appear precisely
under the blue it wants to perish
it has an impassioned soul
it has the wrong head
it wants the open truth
it proclaims in vain
(it will have only half)
as just punishment
the sparrowhawk will eat it.

10
in assenza del fatto
fare un altro fatto
al posto del fatto
un rimedio un baratto
il pensiero da sotto
la notte del gatto
era il mio era il tuo
era il nostro era il suo
se è detto è già fatto
non fare lo stronzo
dimmi la verità
dimmela dimmela.

10
in the absence of the deed
doing another deed
in place of the deed
a remedy a swap
the thought from below
the night of the cat
it was mine it was yours
it was ours it was his
if what's said is already done
don't be an ass
tell me the truth
tell me tell me.

11
chioschetti delle angurie
polverose lampadine
questo tempo a sbafo
così bello così vuoto
se ne va il triciclo dei gelati
(torna l'intero
se tutti sono andati?)
non c'è posto
tra il fatto e finito?
oh grande notte
oltre i fili del tram
stai tu con me - se con nessuno
mi sono smarrito.

11
little watermelon stands
dusty lightbulbs
this scrounging time
so beautiful so empty
the ice cream cart goes away
(will the whole come back
if they're all gone?)
is there no place
between done and finished?
oh great night
beyond the tram wires
stay with me – if with no one
I've become lost.

12
il lavandino al piano di sopra
così vicina mio corpo città
in un soffio
cadono calze di seta
(una fortezza è l'individuo)
(alte cosce e dignità)
(ultime giarrettiere)
(ma voi lucenti stelle e voi
pesanti pianeti - che mai v'incontrate
da vicino)
(invisibili tracolli - vostro astuto piacere)
siate benigni
in questa notte umana
ditele che avvenga il piccolo caos
(un frufru di seta)
un fatto che intercede
forcine di finta tartaruga
i bigodini nel cassetto
aspettare che salga la caffettiera
come doppiare il soggetto.

12
the washbasin on the next floor up
so close my body city
in a hiss
silk stockings fall
(the individual is a fortress)
(tall thighs and dignity)
(last garters)
(but you shining stars and you
heavy planets – who never meet
up close)
(invisible collapses – your cunning pleasure)
may you be indulgent
in this human night
tell her that a little chaos may occur
(a rustling of silk)
an action that intercedes
hairpins of fake tortoise shell
curlers in the drawer
waiting for the percolator to bubble
as if doubling the subject.

13
chi teneva così lucide
le maniglie le porte - con i teli
sulle macchine da scrivere
finita la settimana
a te dieci a te venti
interiori campane - frullini
come un tipo di ali
compra allora accidenti
signora la prego
bottoni mollette
la soffice talpa
vittorioso toccala caro
venditori,
figli di contadini,
cosa fate con dio?

13
those who kept the handles
of the doors so polished – with the covers
on the typewriters
the week ended
ten to you twenty to you
interior bells – whisks
like a sort of wings
wow then purchase
signora I beg you
buttons clothespins
fluffy mole
triumphant touch it expensive
sellers,
peasants' children,
what are you doing with god?

14

                                      (vedi quel fatto laggiù?
                                      vorrei essere là
                                      guardando da qua
                                      non c'è altro modo)

ma
coricato bocconi congiungere
la grande ferita
stellina della sera
tutte le sere mi dico:
quel grido di toccarti
per farti scomparire
gioia evoluta
palpebra di noi due
non temere
la mia parte lontana
che si consuma
mentre l'altra incuriosita
s'avvicina.

14

                                    (see that thing down there?
                                    I'd like to be there
                                    looking from here
                                    there's no other way)

but
laid face down to unite
the great wound
evening star
every night I tell myself:
that cry from touching you
to make you disappear
evolved joy
eyelid of we two
do not fear
my distant part
that consumes itself
while the other made curious
draws nearer.

15
corpi dove vanno così belli
bei denti bandierine
adesso che taci ci siamo
facciamo una verità
non la facciamo?

ormai così lontano dall'inizio
la cosa qual era tenuta d'occhio
è saltata di qua
di là nelle mani - inseguite le mani

moltiplicata da te
per due per tre - cosa bella cosa
se il nome ti acchiappa - ti mette nella pappa
se la cosa acchiappa te - vince il papa vince il re

anche questa volta - impossibile concludere
il presente taglia in mezzo
nemmeno una frase è compiuta
e il corpo?
gli istanti felici?
sono la garanzia
ha detto uno dei banditi

ti sei fermato sulla negazione
(proprio lì ti è successo)
ama non m'ama
è allora che la giostra si è fermata
per ore (oh per ore tutta la nottata)

15
bodies where do they go so beautiful
beautiful teeth flags
now that you're silent here we are
shall we do something truthful
shall we not?

by now so far from the beginning
the thing that eyes had been kept on
leapt from here
to there in their hands – so many hands

multiplied by you
by two by three – thing beautiful thing
if you're caught by the name – you're put in the mush
if you're caught by the thing – the pope and king win

this time as well – impossible to conclude
the present cuts in two
not even a sentence is finished
and the body?
the happy moments?
they are the guarantee
said one of the bandits

you stopped on denial
(it happened to you right there)
he loves me he loves me not
it's then that the merry-go-round stopped
for hours (oh for hours for the entire night)

16
alcune cose alle spalle
non fanno un racconto
(non file di meliga)
(buona pesa è il concreto)
(piantagrane del quantitativo)
salutiamoci qui - fatti vivo

quello che vedi è un buco
un evento tra parole
s'intravvedono belle ginocchia
lasciami restare intendevo

è l'effetto della vicinanza
il primo piano che rende ciechi
rabbiosi tir sulla tangenziale
irrilevante è l'inizio
se tutte le volte cominciamo?

e l'origine?
(così qui - così lontana)
non provarci nemmeno:
è il punto di vista degli uccelli
delle margherite.

16
a few things behind you
don't make a story
(not rows of sorghum)
(the concrete is of good weight)
(nitpicker of the quantitative)
let's say goodbye here – come see me

what you see is a hole
an event between words
beautiful knees can be glimpsed
I meant let me stay

it's the effect of the proximity
the first level that makes you blind
angry truck on the ring road
is the beginning irrelevant
if we are beginning every time?

and the origin?
(so near – so far)
let's not even try
it's the bird's-eye
view of the daisies.

17
erano risposte premature
(senza le domande)
(la voglia di fare crack?)
(sanatoria dell'amore)
(non necessari
nati ugualmente)
(il manchevole
portato con onore)
illimitati (bambini
finite le scuole)
non si può pensare
in motorino
(sia il pensiero che aspetta)
(fintanto
che non abbiamo finito)
ma tu proteggimi
anestesia incosciente
cara mamma madonna
che con il piede
schiacci il tuo serpente!

17
they were premature responses
(without the questions)
(the desire to crack?)
(amnesty of love)
(not necessary
born all the same)
(the imperfect
carried with honor)
unlimited (children
done with school)
you can't even think
on a moped
(it may be the thought that's waiting)
(until
we have finished)
but you protect me
unconscious anesthesia
dear mother madonna
who with your foot
crushes your snake!

18
ci sono altre descrizioni possibili
c'è il tendone del bar (a righe rosse e blu)
si trattengono l'un l'altro - sguardi
ma chi aspetta l'errore?
o capovolgere il rovescio - bella mossa
c'è crisi nel continuo
gridano aiuto le sirene
casi d'urgenza - che portano salvezza
finalmente - oh benvenuta
sulla prua del nulla
sconosciuta!

18
there are other possible descriptions
there's the café awning (with red and blue stripes)
they hold each other back – glances
but who's waiting for the error?
or turning over the other side – nice move
there's crisis in the continuum
the sirens cry for help
urgent matters – that bring salvation
finally – oh welcome woman
on the bow of nothing
unknown!

19
sequestrato in altre storie in famiglie
il distante non è qui
(c'erano accordi tu dici?)
l'educazione del tatto
(sempre un po' indietro
rispetto al desiderio)
oh cielo senza preferenze
luce senza sesso
mente senza sera
guarigione sarebbe un'eclisse
un pube scuro
una nuvola nera.

19
sequestered within other stories
family secrecy
the distant is not here
(there were agreements you say?)
the politeness of tact
(always a little behind
with respect to desire)
oh heaven without preferences
light without sex
mind without evening
recovery would be an eclipse
a dark pubis
a cloud that became black.

20
illimitati esterni
ogni volto dietro finestre
oh voi
abitanti
parole usate in comune
finte porte di casa
fu all'inizio il segreto?
il male neonato
forse tettine
di madri insicure
per avvicinarsi
a quel lontano
andrà solo lontano
il suo cammino?

20
unlimited exteriors
every face behind windows
oh you
inhabitants
words used in common
fake door to the house
was the secret at the beginning?
the evil newborn
maybe the small tits
of insecure mothers
in order to get nearer
that distance
will its path only
go far away?

21
eppure - sono sicuro
è là dentro (il dicibile)
o è qui?
(girando intorno all'isolato)
ti chiedo
(corpo imperscrutabile)
quando alzi le ascelle
(troppo vicina figura)
risorgano
su ammirevoli tacchi
i tuoi passi
slanci
del nostro acclamare
lampioncini di carta
qualcosa che sussiste
senza disperare.

21
and yet – I am sure
it's there inside (the sayable)
or is it here?
(going around the block)
I ask you
(inscrutable body)
when you raise your armpits
(too close a figure)
may they rise
on admirable heels
your steps
surges
of our acclaim
paper Chinese lanterns
something that exists
without despairing.

22
non posso competere
(tu non lasci impronte)
l'inizio è ininterrotto
(più si ripete più si perfeziona)
per questo ti dico
(in questo finto continuo)
(insistenti tram - alba d'inverno)
se all'inizio era no
rimani tutto negato
oppure
arcangelo dell'etica
cosa proponi?
qualcosa di misero?
o una cosa tenera
bambini che tirano
l'orlo della gonna?
ma cosa ne dici
dell'impronta
di un salto mirabile
una lunga sosta a mezz'aria
da acrobata?
invece sconsiglio:
non passare due volte sul negato
(è un finto ponticello)
mai e poi mai
con l'entusiasmo del perdono.

22
I can't compete
(you don't leave impressions)
the beginning is uninterrupted
(the more it's repeated the more it's perfected)
this is why I say to you
(in this fake continuum)
(insistent trams – dawn of winter)
if at the beginning it was no
you remain completely hopeless
or
archangel of ethics
what do you propose?
something miserable
or a tender thing
children who pull
the skirt's hem?
but what do you say
about the impression
of an admirable leap
a long pause in midair
like an acrobat?
instead I advise against it:
don't pass twice over the denied
(it's a fake little bridge)
never ever
with the enthusiasm of forgiveness.

23
non sono fatti
(per tutta la notte
grilli - respiri)
(pensa all'effervescenza)
(all'idrolitina - anni cinquanta
dei contadini)
pensa al mandorlo che fiorì
e sta fiorito di notte
(in quantità enormi - l'accadere)
ma cosa singola (una prova del nove)
(come l'appello - per nome
e cognome)
(il presente è lungo
dal presente non si sbuca)
vai più indietro
se vuoi la foto con tutti
non abbracciare la sua gonna
all'altezza dei ginocchi.

23
they are not done
(for the whole night
strange whims – breaths)
(think of the effervescence)
(of the fizzy drink – from the 1950s
of the country people)
think of the almond tree that flowered
and remained flowering at night
(in enormous quantities – the event)
but a single thing (an acid test)
(like roll call – by first
and last name)
(the present is long
one doesn't emerge from it)
go further back
if you want the photo with everyone
don't hug her skirt
at the level of her knees.

24
l'universale non verrà
(ma non ci lascia le parentesi?)
quindi accecante
rimarrà la luce?
all'interno dei cristalli
comandi secchi - aghi roventi
(oh fantasmi del buio)
(si arrendono
in posizione fetale)
nel falso ventre
(falso rivedere)
(con i minuti contati
dove non si può rimanere).

24
the universal will not come
(but won't it leave us parentheses?)
will the light therefore
remain blinding
within the crystals
dry commands – burning needles
(oh ghosts of the dark)
(they give up
in a fetal position)
in the false belly
(false re-meeting)
(with the counted minutes
where one cannot remain).

The revolving door of the Hotel Excelsior

> *"For the love of God, watch your words."*
> [Johannes Tauler, 14th century]

I think there's a duty to say something, as happens among tables, near the end, when the unfortunate person, by now in dire straits, cannot get out of saying a few words.

I've seen circumstances of this sort, with those honored at work or at celebrations at the end of their careers, with gatherings of relatives and employees, an event taken to its climax, to nowhere so to speak, through an overabundance of presents, a jubilee that begins with seven Piedmontese-style antipasti.

The words that I have the duty to speak do not intend to contribute—as someone might expect—to the strengthening of such festivities but rather, to hastening the consensus of the guests who, unaware, are drawn to an empyrean place, with the appearance of a banquet within which, among the cheers, every party's secret disorientation creeps in.

I mean to say that the conversation that hovers over that hall will show, in a little bit, the character of a tax collector arriving to draw payment, exercising that principle of repetition under which, in vain, living beings beg.

By that, I don't mean to assert that speaking about one person is an offense to the silence of another but rather, that worthy speaking may know, in its heart, to be a passer-by, with the integrity of someone, not yet revealed, who is arriving.

Is it not Emmanuel Lévinas who, echoing some verses of Isaiah, says: "the word *I* means here I am"?

With that, doesn't one intend, perhaps, to assert the primacy of the unexpected which, before recomposing itself, leaves an indelible sign in the air, an empty and poignant stroke with which even language cannot compete?

Similarly, one could—pilfering an image from the young Hegel—hope that language dissolves completely in its own meaning, like a host on the tongue of the faithful, with no residue, such that it does not become a principle of urban planning, a map of Babylon!

In this case, one can note—so as not to encourage hasty conclusions—that this does not entail dissolution of the word and of signs in general, but rather, the humble and unilateral forgetfulness of the faithful, dazed in maximum comprehension of something.

One can observe, in this regard, how the word—as residue, the wood of every shipwreck—is nonetheless a sign that we love: exterior, capable of being recalled, a buoy in the night, and no end of other problems!

The language of the banquet does not have these worries, and taking advantage of the huge meal, it lets its words whirl within the hall, like the wings of doves in old garrets, unpursuable, as if there were no individual ones or only briefly, a general rustling until—now here, now there—the human aviary becomes quiet, as if requesting an intervention from above, a liquidation, a desire to be silenced, to be told objectively, objectivized and finally subdued, as if all the words already spoken in vain had unanimously asked to recognize, publicly, the reason for the gathering.

It is then that the awaited speech begins, lurching, thinning out the spontaneous fervor among the last sounds of forks rested on the plate or silently on the tablecloth, while waved-away waitresses—latecomers—remain standing, immobile, supporting a stack of dessert plates not deposited in time in front of the dinner guests' polished avoirdupois.

These waitresses are caught by the speech while, not yet having shrunk into their position of listening near the door to the kitchen, they seem to be surprised, half-way there, on their feet with their miniskirts and long legs among the words, almost unredeemed bodies.

The question could be resolved or mitigated by the speaker who slows the sentence, giving time to the unfortunate to slip away, but that does not exempt the bystanders, seated and ready to listen, rigid like all followers, from perceiving those standing girls as an inconvenient and awkward interference, live beings in the house of the concept.

I do not intend to take advantage of living beings who generate bubbles within any sort of sentence, nor do I love complaining about language that stretches to its own limit, to the nothingness of everything long surpassed, nor am I moved by its contradicting itself, the nostalgia of being an occurrence and, as such, longing to die. Nor, finally, do I want to be moved while it sacrifices itself in some way, civilly, drawing violence into the sentence instead of directly onto the victims, like when the browned and crackling fat of the big oxen flows in cruel slaughters.

With regard this image of the sacrifice—improvident, one might say, precisely in the middle of a banquet—I think it's the duty of every dinner guest to give a thought to the encouragement with which, on the evolutionary scale, each being supports the next, not for harmony nor as a eucharistic gift, but for the advantage of strength, of its exception consciously rendered legal.

It is through opportunity and the servility of rhetoric that, in favor of banquets, there is taken from the animal, having passed through dark slaughterhouses, the name if its living origins, with *guancialino* in the place of jaw, little hoof, giblets, livers, offal, breasts,* to say nothing of the seven cuts of boiled meat, served on a trolley, all of them named and one by one, according to an irrefutable primacy of the word, which grants an unheard-of peace, a consoling anesthesia, to all those members.

Continuing on this theme, I witnessed the memorable scene of a butcher who was caressing the beast's head, straightening the short curls of blond fur and who, in the end, resting a hand on its forehead with persuasive words, with the other launched the stupefying blow which, like in a gag of the inept, before penetrating the animal's cranium, hit the skin held between the thumb and index finger of the consoling hand, fortunately grazing it, as a result of which the hand was withdrawn with a jerk, but immediately afterward, faithful in compassion, it accompanied the beast toward its dreadful fall.

The butcher, at that point, pulled out his handkerchief and wrapped it around his bleeding hand, but with nothing broken, as if that were the way the poetics were supposed to work.

This speech began, as was said, with the extinguishing of the last spontaneous words, but that apex of the banquet, which seemed to be leading to legal language, turned out to be a bluff, and the speech showed itself, when it was all over, to be an addendum, a marginal note, to the point that the more it went on, full of *Positivität* (= the *datum mortuum* of something), the more that seemed to apply, without consulting the expressive looks of those present, the devices and tics of the sentences born with sovereign power, with memories of decisions, of judgements, of impediments through which everyone remembers having cried, as a child, when the tears—salty, having fallen down their cheeks—joined with little rivulets within reach of the tongue, a moment in which the child, through instinct, almost inevitably licks them, finds them good and stops crying, as if he had had an inspiration.

---

* Translator's note: The Italian terms for all of these parts, once prepared, carry diminutive suffixes: *guancialino, piedino, durelli, fegatini, coratella, puntine.*

Woe unto the orator who triggers such images, since his destiny is marked, as a general suspicion spreads through the hall, an alert to that which, instead of assuaging the individuals with mastery of sweetness—art that has the language delivered word for word, as in love—it looms over them, rendering them irritated and noisy, someone moving their chair, someone picking up their napkin, someone knocking against a tinkling glass as if it were made of crystal.

And me?

I, like everyone, faced with the terminal escalation of the enormous sentence, am seeking, within myself, a pause with which I am familiar, a sort of shaky opening, like when confronting an awkward step.

If I look at the diners, they all seem to me to be wandering within their pause, a sort of train station waiting room at night, and all of them seem to me to be facing that step that leads to the word coming up, patiently.

What is there within that pause?

Our opaque body, its three-dimensionality that cannot be summed up, the timidity of the word, an excess that makes us large while, conversely, poor in expression?

Among all the pauses, one looms motionless and dark: it is the pause with just one side, a primitive one, in defense of our birth, interruption and principal beginning, the mother pause, thought at the back of my neck.

Does there derive from that irreparable side of our pause the attempt to reverse it in front of us, as a positive element, in the same way that a hole is positive, a place where language weaves its reparative canvas?

Is that the pitiful error that leads us to the machinations of inner life?

Faced with that closed door, does language learn discontinuity, the daring passage to the negative, such that all speaking must be born, humanely, from the depths of supplication?

Thus, for men, is every clear display always a outcome (*exitus exilium*)—not a given, but rather, a result?

Does the pause require the art of unlearning, the delicate task of forgetting, a virtue that, with respect to semiotic abilities, wafts an ethical and mystical perfume, as Roland Barthes seems to assert on the last page of 1977's *Leçon inaugurale*?

Giacomo Leopardi holds that in some cases—in birds, for example—what is created is not an expression as much as an expressiveness, freed from the control of the results and therefore, an anarchical and completely inventive language, of pure instinct and pure liberation. At least that's what I seem to understand when he asserts that birds "abound beyond measure in extrinsic life" (*Operette morali, Elogio degli uccelli*).

And he continues: "And since they abound in extrinsic life, they are in a like manner rich in their interior, but in a way that such abundance results in their benefit and delight, as with little children."

Does the birds' bliss, without any other task than the goodness of existing (*respicite volatilia coeli; considerate lilia agri...*) represent, miraculously, the language of the pause?

Is it the pause that destabilizes the very idea of form, so as to not leave us alone and merely represented? Is the pause, then, maternal, an untouchable womb?

While he praises the happy birds beyond all prudence, Leopardi does not, however, seem to want to become one of them, except as a wish, the best way for retracting.

In fact, Leopardi says, "I would like"; he says, "for a little bit of time"; he says, to be precise: "...similarly I would like, for a little bit of time, to be turned into a bird, to feel that happiness and joy of their life."

He does not say that he would like to reject the division between his own voice and his own being—our extreme, fraudulent revenge. On the contrary, he says he would like a fixed-term experiment, with the aim of feeling, at least once, what it is to exist in a pure state.

To give an idea of that extraordinary experience, to learn, as Höderlin wrote, from the nightingales (*bei Nachtigallen zu lernen*), Leopardi advises the state of drunkenness, even alcoholic, the exercise of laugher like someone slamming the door noisily, beyond language or (an extreme resource) madness.

Here: "...considering that men, unhappy as they are above all other animals, they are likewise delighted more than any other, by every untroubling alienation of mind, by forgetfulness of themselves, by the intermission of life, so to speak, through which either by interrupting themselves or, for a time, diminishing their feeling and awareness of their own wrongs, they receive no small benefit."

Alienation, forgetfulness, intermission: is this how one can experience pure meaning, without the sign that blackmails it or holds it back, extended a little bit, an opening in which loss and fear creep in?

Might it be the body that becomes a sign?

Is it to be hoped, physically, that the body could be so much in the open, without a hiding place, while it was always seeking an alibi so as not to be caught out, a target that might be knocked down?

Or is it relearning from childhood? From the courage of children who want to speak?

The child, the national little boy, would not, in any event, be under the aegis of innocence, but rather, involved in a rite of initiation in which he offers his own body to language, tragically, imploring the teacher so that when he is accepted, he will then be transformed, advancing in loss, learning consolation without shame.

Does the very young and somewhat clever child represent the state that the poet must reach with cunning and discipline? This is not a new idea, and there must be a reason.

Might one assert, then, that effective experimentation of language does not occur consequently and fully within language, as an exercise, but rather between language and body, as destiny or destination?

There's conclusive evidence that determines the powers of language, and it's the injunction to stop! caused by pain—which is not communicable—nor, by embracing the suffering person, will someone feel his hurt.

Pain stops at the borders of the individual, and magically, during the long nights, leaves all others in peace.

It's when faced with pain that language gives in to being a symbol and pro forma so that, in the stress of the blow, it distances itself feverishly, as if hyperbole were a lament.

The experience I would like to pose as an example concerns the Gospel of John, in the easy Latin of high school.

Everything happened together, in those years of magic: my love for "Madonna dir vo' voglio," by Jacopo da Lentini and for Jesus Christ.

What struck me, in the Gospel of John, was in reality just one word with two faces, like the signal of a traffic officer.

The occasion is that of the dialogue between Jesus and Nicodemus, one night in early spring.

It is not important, here, to know what they said in detail. Important was a verb, in its passive form: *Et sicut Moyses exaltavit serpentum in deserto, ita exaltari oportet Filium hominis* (John 3:14).

The serpent to which Jesus is referring is the copper serpent raised on a stake in the time of Moses, the vision of which would have healed the bite of real snakes (Numbers 21:4-9).

An ugly premonition accompanies the passive form of the verb *exaltari*, which, although trying to present itself with its celebratory face, does not succeed in masking the anxiety of the passive, the experiencing and suffering.

The even greater magnificence of the passive, like the beloved being, becomes, not by chance—as Dante teaches—an exacting request that does not "forgive," revealing itself as an enigmatic gift, an obligation taken on in sleep, through which grace falls into the sphere of recompense, once and for all, as the famous verse states: "Love, which pardons no one loved from loving" (*Inferno* V:103).

It was to be expected that the traffic officer's signal would turn around, and the horror would appear: *et ego, si exaltatus fuero a terra, omnes traham ad meipsum. Hoc autem dicebat signficans, qua morte esset moriturus* (John 12:32-33).*

Behind that *exaltari* there was this: suspension between heaven and earth—without, however, having the gift of lightness, without the support of one's feet, the way in which the living circumvent gravity.

Could it be that poetry is a *suspended* language, raised symbolically like the copper serpent, finally raised live, on its own, like a destiny of the messiah, not to represent the event, but to be its cry?

Is there, in poetry's nature, an intrinsic passivity, an awareness without the distraction of acting, a knowledge engraved on the page of glass?

*

It was not expected that the idea of a pause would lead me to these intolerable images, all the more so considering that speech, while it accepts the power of the pause, endorses rejection of 51% of itself, placing itself—as speech—in a lesser position, ready to offer its throat.

Can the revenge of gravity, which torments a suspended body, be compared, nonetheless, to the justicialism of speech that does not forgive the pause's insubordination?

Is it the pause, then, that applies an immense gravity to the words, understanding their weight, literally, as poetry's words want to be heavy?

Is this the meaning of leave-taking, which leads back every time to the dissolution of an undertaking, when its meaning is given off, reaching its peak?

An image accompanies me that I cannot silence: I see, from behind, figures of words that are moving away—what's more, toward the west. Feminine words—literally, women words, in conformity with their grammatical gender.

---

* "'And I, when I am lifted up from the earth, will draw all people to myself.' He said this to indicate the kind of death he was to die."

They do not speak with me. I can only call them, just once.

They don't resemble in any way the words of the banquet, which instead move on, meeting halfway, drawing agreement.

My beloved words don't seek my agreement. I only see the backs of their necks. I also, I confess, feel the back of my neck, the empty threshold from which I derive.

Can one only begin from the beginning, as if history were an accumulation that does not satisfy the requirements of purity?

The purity that I mean does not concern the plundering of waste through denials and refusals but rather, the ability to make of the *improper* a great celebration of the spirit, an abundance that does not shrink back so that the pure may "represent itself only in the impure" (Hölderlin, *Letter to Friedrich Neuffer*, 12 November 1798).

In a poem, it's the departure that counts, especially the fake departure, the true gem of every verse, so that the poem may unrestrainedly carry out the salvation of error, its pride.

The immediacy of a poem is the result of a twist: the side of our neck does not let itself be tricked.

In a text from a few years ago, written for the anthology, *Those Who from Afar Look Like Flies*, edited by Luigi Ballerini, Beppe Cavatorta, and Gianluca Rizzo, with regard to *child theory*, I quoted Saint Augustine, availing myself of him in the following way:

"The existence of the other side, an ordinary fact in solid geometry, introduces, to the primary question of 'side of the shoulders,' that which pushes us onto the scene, leaving us, in plain view, with a 'single side.'"

Every event occurs from a single side, a position of solitude and the reason for compassionate tics, like someone going more than once around a cube. It is difficult, for example, under those conditions, to catch poetry red-handed.

Regarding sides, of those in shadow and their relationship to language, I would like to state that with respect to language, I have always been attracted by its being origin (behind) and goal (in front), thereby taking on the nature of a perpetual conversion.

One admirable conversion is that described by Saint Augustine (*Confessions*, VIII, 7.16), in which it seems feasible to abandon one side and find oneself face-to-face. Augustine addresses God, saying to Him: "you bent me over myself (*retorquebas me ad me ipsum*), pulling me from behind myself (*auferens me a dorso meo*), where I had hidden in order not to know myself (*ubi me posu-*

eram, dum nolle me attendere), and you saw to it that I would look myself in the face (*et constituebas me ante faciem meam...*)."

We're dealing with a contortionist's position, the result of an exaggerated awareness, so as to place oneself in a zenith position, without sides, going beyond poetry with sanctity.

Although my idea of poetry may always have been animated by a desire for conversion, implicit in the language itself, in its unsteady and changeable character, I will confess that I never imagined to be able to avoid the slope, the strenuous resistance to maintaining a position that was failing.

That was the shock from which *child theory* was born.

If it was a case of unmasking, then it was a face that was transforming into the ultimate mask, without protection, the ultimate substitution, the strange spin of the merry-go-round.

An empty place, on one side or the other, may have migrated under the impulse of the verses, like a circulating nothing. I'll allow myself, in this regard, to quote an expression, for me enigmatic, of Dante Alighieri—one which, however, I feel to be heavy with suggestions regarding "discordance [*discorde*]," that which is never absolved and that incites language:

"With regard to parisyllabic verses, they are used only rarely because of their roughness. In fact, they maintain the nature of even numbers, which submit to odd numbers just as material submits to form." (*De vulgari eloquentia*, II, 5.7)

The unparisyllabic nature of poetry, the fundamental disparity of existing—oh the powerful remedies, the impulses—have persuaded me through the decades to consider individual poems as pieces of wreckage, something that, presenting themselves as completed, took away from me the faculty of voice, the possibility of conversion, the remedy with which, mercifully, to re-establish a degraded origin.

When is it that a text becomes fixed like a fossil?

When, in the process of reduction to a formula, did it arrive equal to zero—that is, to be pure form?

Is a poem always a cameo, something that challenges any space and offers itself at the limit, the glory of individual beings?

Or does a form always contain its own fear—that is, its own criticism?

My comfort is in the following sentence: ...*ich werde mich immer und immer wieder berichtigen müssen, um der Wahrheit zu geben, was der Wahrheit ist.* / *[I will have to again and again put myself right, so that I may give to the truth what is owed to it.]* (Georg Trakl, *Letter to Erhard Buschbeck*, 1912).

Does *berichtigen* mean continually improving collateral opportunities, arriving, in the end, against oneself, where we will be, as broken-hearted beings, without the quantitative resources of error?

Does going against oneself mean making oneself speak to the point of being knocked down? – let's let language rage upon us until it transfigures and disfigures, until the fateful word, until the varnished nothing, oh Gottfried Benn!

I don't intend, here, to confess why—as soon as a poem ends—I might have gone back to redo it, to repeat it. I wouldn't know.

Did I love the pause more than its impairment through words?

Did I rewrite the words to revise that pause?

Against the threat of the scribe, he who bears witness upon me for purposes of judgement, *liber scriptus proferetur...*(Dies irae), did I, by writing, perhaps embark upon a perpetual beginning that offers, once again, an excuse for error to the point of prescription (as that's interpreted in court): pardon for the aforesaid and an admonition to every writer: that the text might be like the shadow of the hand?

Doesn't something of this sort happen in stanza number five of *Brot und Wein/Bread and Wine* by Hölderlin, on page seven of the great Homburg notebook (*Frankfurter Ausgabe*, volume 6, 1976)?

It has always made me happy to see the philologists be at a loss. Is valid poetry that which calls itself, in its legal form, poetry?

Does there need to be a formal act of proprietorship, so as to demonstrate that it's a matter of business, not of a gift?

Does poetry, as something finite, not tolerate the idle word that arrives at the end, absent-mindedly, that which paces itself among the verses, literally between one line and another?

The problem is not the variant—entertainment for the philologists—but rather the presence, in the text, of this wandering word: always expected, and that arrived before the already closed expression.

To what text belong *Weiß ist der Augenblik/White is the moment* and *Fast triffet den Rükken das Glük/Joy seems to strike from behind*?

In what relation do these fateful words stand with the text already copied out, which everyone had accepted as the Hölderlin's "property"?

Relegated to the machinery of criticism, can they perhaps ever be considered as constellations of the text—its moons—which the text drags through its own sky?

Does the text include its moons?

Is the text a planetary system?

Does the text know which shining bodies might pass, every night, to illuminate its darkness?

Or could we imagine an unlimited text, suffering from charitable viruses that—in fever, like a leavening—induce language to say and resay itself, a perpetual trial among the interruptions of the bodies, an expression of the end of the world?

*

The text that concludes, in a final way, becomes responsible not only for the conclusion, but even more for its beginning, however far off.

Between beginning and end, there is released—if all goes well—the greatest grammatical consensus, an unbreakable alliance, irreproachable language that exposes itself without fear, forever.

With that, in my small way, I mean to give honor to completed poems, to the sonnet that if, as a test, some thoughtless person might want to tamper with it, one word after another might collapse on its own, exactly like a house of cards.

But I am not the sonnet, but rather its pause that ignites excitedly, like a fan of spirit, making confetti fly.

My task is to provide the error, subjected to justification, bringing forth wreckage.

This is why, every time, I have upended the text's knitting through childlike curiosity, through incredulity, through penitence—thwarting the hard face of the expression to find the mysterious appeal, without the protection of outside facts, without exclusive and ruinous histories confronting the cry of the mind.

The upended knitting has allowed me to imagine a world that does not deny what it hides, that preserves its incredible reserve of figures, that loves its accomplices, the knots and threads that dangle, the nape of the neck—I would dare say, my maternity.

Like someone who, hearing knocking or with a premonition, goes out the door and, in that position, covers the view of the interior, thereby showing himself both as a sign of obstruction and a hasty response, have I always heard my poems running on the threshold of the verse, like an empty declaration, dulled by their task, showing empty hands?

Those verses that obstructed the entrance, *en déshabillé*, whether they were facing outward or inward, were the verses of the threshold: a passage, a liability like the position of someone praying whose speech, since it's an active prayer, affirms only what is missing.

Through all the years spent with poetry—and even now—I distinguish two types of affirmations. One (stupid) is that which takes over—I have always seen it in the company of drunkards. The other (anguished) is that which, as it affirms, becomes excessive, the product of a hyperbole that doesn't make them larger, but more out of place, broader, and more distant.

I would say that between the affirmation of taking over and the hyperbolic affirmation, there runs the same difference as that between the unpleasant univocal (the reason for misunderstandings) and empty meaning (the reason for brotherhood).

It is useless to say that I was always on the side of the hyperbolic affirmation, launched to chase the projection of the text in the wake of unhinged words only seemingly free but in reality, heavy bodies nervous about the flight, about the precipice.

Could there exist a poetry that is like a collision with language, a movement without any other following it, a primary poetry, a proto-poetry?

Was secondary poetry, then, under these conditions, that which went beyond the stopping line, that which, instead of a countermeasure—its truth—relied on justification, on the excuses of the facts, on similarities, and on confabulation?

Very little remained for poetry under that plan of sanctity: a beginning, an impulse, an overwhelmed thought.

Did every word have to pay the penalty of its own daring and return, from an uncertain sign, to the mute companion of living, to the point of departure that was screaming like a newborn?

If poetry is the imprint of the athletic shoe before the jump (through which never, from those signs, would one know if the jump really occurred, let alone successfully), there does not remain to the poet—to me in this case, if I can define myself as such, practicing the profession insistently—anything but going back over that first stretch of the run, endlessly, searching not for the true that justifies, but the false that guesses.

A dark suspicion beset me in childhood when the fairy tale, in Perrault's version, which reached even the Piedmontese countryside on winter evenings, related how Tom Thumb, after pebbles and lacking anything else, had left a trail of breadcrumbs that were promptly pecked up by the sparrows.

Tom Thumb's biggest worry, at that point of the story, was not finding home—a remote possibility—but of finding the signs, an immediate presence.

The disappearance of the signs was the reasoning for continuously leaving some of them around by crumbling pieces of bread—meagre signs at the end of his resources, crumbs of entreaty.

At this point, one could assert that the verse, born to appease some anxiety, an unmentionable secret, notices very soon that it has no prey to throw itself upon, no real gazelle for the tiger's desire.

Having become its own prey, it dwells within the pause as its refuge, a place of repetitions, echoes, and embarrassing advances.

By that I mean to say that the pause does not produce the silence but rather, the voice that contrasts with it, the shouting of the expression, the most regrettable positivity.

I said shouting not light-heartedly, and I said positivity—that is to say, the hegemony of affirmation, against which the verse had, ideally, risen up—so that all the simple things could flow directly, like an intravenous drip, thereby inserting the poem into the field of hospital care.

The original pause, in reality, seemed to maneuver the circus leash for the wild animal that was returning to my feet, the spotted leopard subdued to the reasonings of style, dangerously docile.

Had language, as a false promise, been brought back to the law of the minimum—that which, in agrarian sciences, limits the powers of nutritional substances?

According to that principle, represented didactically by a vat with one bottom crosspiece lower than the others, the more abundant substance is utilized in the manner and within the limits of the poorer substance, which acts as regulator of thousand-year-old behaviors, the sign of a disconcerting equity of nature, an instantaneous self-limitation, a perennial repentance, in order to humiliate naïve falsehood. Was this what Anaximander meant in his glorious fragment, which says that everything existing pays the penalty of its own daring?

Was the minimum the maximum reached by the living? Was poetry a question of minimums?

Following that principle, was the limit of language existence?

Inevitably the third part, existence would never have been the prêt à porter of the phrase but rather, its resisting boundaries against which language would shatter—shining, if you will.

Was this the deep meaning of Arnaut Daniel's verses?
c'ades, ses lei, dic a lei cointos motz:
pois can la vei non sai, tant l'ai, que dire.

that now, from afar, I imagine crazy words:
then face to face, I am so much within her, I no longer know what to say.

Although *Sobrafan*, the fanaticism for feeling and saying, generates the excellent excesses of the *sestina*, does it not perhaps express an immediate contrition, a burning envy when confronted with a "composition with silences", just as when confronted with the pause of bodies?

Is it for these reasons that I returned to my poems like a cavalcade of Mongols in a field of corn? Was demolition the task of poetry?

Is it only in this way that the dialectic exclamation, the marvelous puzzle, is rendered possible?

Was remaking the poems like bombing Berlin?

In the photos from 1945, you can see through the facades that were still standing; you can see empty windows like pure frames. Ants of pure life wander about among the mounds of debris, very quickly arranged—a new order, like the ghost of its construction.

Books published by Agincourt Press in the Opuntia Series

Giorgio Bassani, *The Collected Poems*, translated, with an introduction and notes by Roberta Antognini and Peter Robinson (2023)

Laura Liberale, *Thanato-Aesthetics*, translated by Murtha Baca and Federica Santini (2023)

John Latta, *Some Alphabets*, with an introduction by Mark Scroggins (2022)

Gianfranco Contini, *An Idea of Dante*, translated by Stephen Sartarelli (2021)

Giani Stuparich, *One Year of School and The Island*, translated by Charles Klopp and Melinda Nelson, with an introduction by Charles Klopp (2021)

Michela Dall'Aglio, *In the Beginning There Was Freedom: An Itinerary between Science, Philosophy, and Faith*, translated by Thomas Haskell Simpson (2020)

Mariano Bàino, *Yellow Fax and Other Poems* (2019)

Alfredo Giuliani (ed.), *I Novissimi: Poetry for the Sixties*, edited by Luigi Ballerini and Federica Santini (2017)

Gianluca Rizzo (ed.), *On the Fringe of the Neoavantgarde / Ai confine della neoavanguardia, Palermo 1963 – Los Angeles 2013* (2017)

Massimo Ciavolella and Gianluca Rizzo (ed.), *Savage Words: Invectives as a Literary Genre* (2016)

Massimo Ciavolella and Gianluca Rizzo (ed.), *Like Doves Summoned by Desire: Dante's New Life in 20th Century Literature and Cinema. Essays in memory of Amilcare Iannucci* (2012)

Adriano Spatola, The Porthole, translated by Beppe Cavatorta and Polly Geller (2011)

Maurizio Cucchi, *The Missing*, translated with an introduction by Gianpiero W. Doebler (2008)

Elio Pagliarani, *The Girl Carla and Other Poems* (2009)

Remo Bodei, *We, The Divided: Ethos, Politics, and Culture in Post-War Italy, 1943-2006* (2006)

Standard Shaefer, *Water & Power* (2005)

Robert Crosson, *The Day Sam Goldwyn Stepped off the Train* (2004)

Paul Vangelisti, *Embarrassment of Survival* (2001)